CW00631683

Islam and The New Totalitarianism
fundamentalism's threat to world civilisation

Robert Corfe is well-qualified as the author of this book on the problem of contemporary Islam. As a businessman working in the Middle East, he has long had successful contacts with Gulf Arabs and other Islamic peoples in the region as well as back home in Britain. As an established author of repute he is well known for his books, *Deism and Social Ethics, The Democratic Imperative, Populism Against Progress, The Future of Politics,* and his works on social capitalism. The present book is a penetrating study of Islamic society and the psychosis that can arise through excess religiosity. Comparisons are made with other societies in the past that have found themselves in a similar situation with Islam today, and in this the author finds hope for a harmonious settlement in the future between the Islamic and non-Islamic worlds.

By the same author –

Islam and the New Totalitarianism

fundamentalism's threat to world civilisation

Robert Corfe

Arena Books

Copyright © Robert Corfe 2016

The right of Robert Corfe to be identified as author of this book
has been asserted in accordance with the Copyright, Designs and
Patents Act 1988.

First published in 2016 by Arena Books

Arena Books
6 Southgate Green
Bury St. Edmunds
IP33 2BL

www.arenabooks.co.uk

All rights reserved. Except for the quotation of short passages for the
purposes of criticism and review, no part of this publication may be
reproduced, stored in a retrieval system, or transmitted, in any form or
by any means, electronic, mechanical, photocopying, recording or
otherwise, without the prior permission of the publisher.

Corfe, Robert- 1935
Islam and the New Totalitarianism *fundamentalism's threat to world*
civilisation

ISBN-13   978-1-909421-77-6

BIC categories:- JFFD, JFFE, JFFL, JFFP, JFSL1, JFSR, JPF, JPFR, HRAP,
                  HRA, HRAB, HRAC.

Printed and bound by Lightning Source UK

Cover design
by Jason Anscomb

Typeset in
Times New Roman

PREFACE

The Islamic threat is possibly the most disturbing political issue in the world today – disturbing in the sense that the fear of consequences impacts more directly on the lives of ordinary people than any other problem. The issue is unusual in that the grounds for conflictual differences are unclear and undefined, but they nonetheless exist in actuality.

It is not as if a war had been declared between two parties and each comprehended the enmity of the other. The origin of the *conflict* (for it is that) is the cultural incompatibility between two civilisations, and the pretence of the deferring party that all differences may be dissolved simply through a policy of multiculturalism. If the latter arose through benevolent conviction as the only perceived path towards peaceful coexistence, leading hopefully to cultural absorption, after a number of years it changed into doubt and then into an illusion, and finally today it is little more than polite pretence.

The issue is more commonly described as "religious," which it is, but in a stricter sense it is cultural. This is because Islam, especially through the propagation of Wahabism, the most powerful force within the faith today, makes no distinction between the secular and the divine. The entire thinking and lifestyle and behaviour of Muslims is directed by religious demands to the exclusion of anything that may be defined as secular or profane – the latter being the preferred pejorative term for what is not authorised by the faith. Such a mindset established by the Prophet Mohammed and his followers, is long enshrined in tradition, and remains to the present day. God is therefore the one authority, and his commands are interpreted through text alone in conjunction with the recorded traditions of the Sunnah or Hadith.

The above conditions, particularly as manifested through the strict puritanical Islam as imposed by Saudi Arabia on a worldwide scale, ensures that the faith is a totalitarian movement. This means that secular reason, or that not taken from holy script is taken as irrelevant and undesirable as a basis for discussion. All totalitarian societies have a fear of contamination and usually take extreme measures to safeguard their internal security. When these do not take the form of barring the entry of foreigners, as in Saudi Arabia, they take the form of arresting and imprisoning dissidents and other suspects. There is consequently no working Islamic democracy anywhere in the Middle East.

The problem in the non-Islamic world, especially in Western Europe, is the penetration of nation states by a religious totalitarianism attempting to impose its proselytising ideology on democratic societies. The variety of means in attempting to achieve this, and the subtlety of the methods, are described in this book. One rationale of Muslims in attempting to justify their approach is the false assumption that Europe is "no longer Christian," and hence the assumed right to imposing the priority of their own religion within a vacuum. The greatest objection of non-Muslims, however, to the penetration of their culture is the creation of alternative legal structures, or a state within the state, as their own "parliament," or internal consultative committees, or the announcement of no-go zones in major cities of the north, or the establishment of Sharia law and Sharia courts as if they held legal authority.

It is only in the wake of terrorist outrages that peoples across Europe have suddenly awoken to the above factors, and are now intent on regaining or defending what might be lost in the near future. If Muslims resist the idea of integration – which they are – then only two alternatives remain: they must either create their own mini-states within the state, or else attempt by subtler means to seize control of leading administrative institutions. Their failure to assimilate can drive them in no other direction. Muslims in Britain are actively engaged in both the above alternatives, as witnessed by their numbers and close cooperation in both the Commons and the Lords, and their power in local government councils nationwide.

The need to associate the identity between the problem of terrorist outrages and that of cultural integration into the nation state is becoming increasingly apparent. This is because of the process of radicalisation of young people and their flight to Syria to join Isis or similar groups, and the recent attempts of European governments to counter these moves. Most shocking of all is the silence of Muslims in response to terrorism. It is as if they were fearful of speaking out on the grounds of compromising the credibility of Islam, or purely through embarrassment at the incidents themselves. In a more perfect world I would expect leading Muslims to speak out loud and clear against terrorist acts, and to openly admit there is something *very wrong with Islam* that allows and encourages such outrages. I would expect such leaders to initiate an open discussion on the criticism of Islam in inviting proposals for necessary reform as a minimum gesture.

This is an urgent book with a threefold purpose: firstly, to analyse the incompatibility between two contrasting civilisations and the consequences; secondly, to examine the possibilities for the cultural integration of Muslims into non-. Islamic societies; and thirdly, to present tentative cultural and religious reforms for Islam at its centre for harmonious relationships in the future.

The approach is sociological and objective, and comparisons are made with other cultures in history that have experienced similar situations to that of Islam today. For example, the second chapter of this book is entitled, *Europe's Age of Religious Shame*. The root cause of Islam's problems is uncovered early in this book, and it is a question of excess religiosity and the psychosis resulting from such a condition. This immediately raises the issue of the author's religious stance in writing this book. Clearly such a book would be unacceptable in the Islamic world if it were written by an atheist or even by an agnostic.

The author admits to a modern approach to religion and a belief in God, and would best describe himself as a Deistic Anglican. That is, he adopts a figurative rather than a literal interpretation of the Bible and theological doctrine, which is probably already in alignment with the views of the majority of ministers ordained in the Church of England at the present day.

He therefore supports a rational or Enlightenment approach to religion with its social bonding benefits, whilst repudiating mysticism, revelation, or anything tending towards excessive religiosity.

In my view, moderate religion is not only benign but a social necessity in a sound society, whilst that bordering on fanaticism, although it cannot be expunged entirely, is harmful, and if widespread, can become a psychological poison in undermining the sanity of a people. The above may be dismissed as personal prejudice, but as issues for discussion they cannot be avoided in considering the problem of contemporary Islam, for the latter is pure religion without a secular dimension.

Lastly, and in support of my authority in writing this book, I must admit that through a long business career, I have had close and friendly relationships with Islamic people, mostly Gulf Arabs, for many years, and with whom I must have discussed religious issues for well over a hundred hours in total. If in the dissertation that follows, I have omitted to raise relevant aspects of the problem on one of the most disturbing political questions of our time, I would be grateful if these were eventually brought to my attention.

CONTENTS

CHAPTER 1
The Threat to World Civilisation

"A religion that is jealous of the variety of learning, discourse, opinions, and sects, as misdoubting it may shake the foundations, or that cherisheth devotion upon simplicity and ignorance, as ascribing effects to the immediate working of God, is adverse to knowledge."

Sir Francis Bacon, *Of the Interpretation of Nature*, chapter 25.

The Problem of Islamic terrorism is more deep-rooted than most of our political leaders are ready to admit. Added to this complexity is the fixed response of Muslims to every violent outrage, in that it "has nothing whatsoever to do with Islam," as Islam is a "religion of peace."

This simple statement of denial, with all its suggested complacency, contradicts the reality for a host of reasons, for every act of terrorism has *everything* to do with mainstream Islam if not directly then indirectly. Until such time as Muslims are prepared to condemn, loud and clear, the extreme nature of Islamic religiosity as manifested at the present time, all must be held as in some way complicit for the horrors that have appalled the world in the present century. Passivity in the face of crime is alone sufficient for condemnation.

The perception which a people, or an organisation religious or otherwise has of itself, is always as it *should be*, or would like to portray itself, rather than as it actually is. When, therefore, accusations of outrage are made, the usual defensive response is to cite the "written word" from a hallowed constitutional document or a holy script to correct a wrong impression, but such a stance is invalidated when it is borne in mind that deeds override theories on what is right or wrong. The judgement of individuals or groups should be based on actions rather than on words. Hence when an organisation is responsible for a violent outrage, it is not sufficient for the individual to distance him- or herself by such disassociating statements as, "Not in my name," or, "This is not in accord with the principles of my religion." Exculpation of the individual can only be achieved through a close analysis of causes followed by the application of a practical and satisfactory long-term resolution of the underlying problem.

The outrages of the past 16 years are nothing new to the history of the Islamic faith, for Islam was born through violence and the use of the sword. Even the intentional destruction of cultural monuments has precedents from the earliest epoch. The desecration of the Bamiyan Buddhas in Afghanistan, or the burning of the irreplaceable library of the Ahmed Baba Institute in Mali, or more recently, the demolition of the major artefacts of Palmyra, are traceable to the earliest barbaric deeds of religious totalitarianism. As soon as the Islamic horde emerged from the sandy wastes of Arabia in conquering Egypt, in 634 AD they destroyed the greatest library of the ancient world.

The justification of the conqueror, Oman, who in the words of Gibbon, "was inspired by the ignorance of a fanatic,"[1] in consigning the Alexandrian Library to the flames was that, "if these writings agree with the book of God, they are useless and need not be preserved; if they disagree, they are pernicious and ought to be destroyed." Over a period of six months this priceless legacy of literature, philosophy, history and science was consigned to the furnaces heating the 4,000 baths of the city, and the greater part of the genius of the ancient world and our Western heritage was lost forever.

This is not to suggest that Islam continued as a force of barbarism throughout its history. Whilst its birth and early development was characterised by an uncompromising totalitarianism, the Arab conquerors became a minority amongst more advanced peoples in the Middle East and across North Africa and were soon culturally absorbed by influences that attracted their better instincts. During the Dark Ages of European history with the fall of the Roman Empire, they cultivated a superior civilisation, particularly in the fields of philosophy, medicine, mathematics, and science which eventually was inherited by the peoples of the West.

---

[1] *History of The Decline & Fall of the Roman Empire*, cap. 51.

With the fall of Abbasid power in Baghdad, and that of the Moors in North West Africa, as Spain regained its lost territory, Islamic political power fell to the Turkic and Ottoman peoples. The latter achieved a glorious flowering in the 16th and 17th centuries before falling into a slow but irreversible political and cultural decline, as the "Sick man of Europe." From the end of the Crusades, in indecisive attempts by the West to recover the Holy Land for the Christian cause, i.e. from the closing decades of the 13th century to those of the 20th, it may be said that a confrontational but distant relationship existed between the European and Islamic worlds. This took the form of a political but not a religious confrontation even though broad cultural differences were recognised on both sides. This is partly illustrated by the fact that France, for example, cultivated a friendly relationship with the Ottoman empire during the period when she was in conflict with the Austrian Habsburgs in the 17th and 18th centuries; or when Germany cultivated friendship with the Turks in seeking to counter-balance Britain's influence in the Middle East at the end of the 19th and start of the 20th centuries.

By the end of the 20th century a total transformation had occurred in the politico-cultural relationships between the Islamic and non-Islamic worlds as a direct economic consequence of the internal combustion engine. The Arabian peninsula had been the birthplace and had always remained the true religious heartland of Islamic civilisation. In addition, Arabia had remained a closed and introverted culture, forbidding to those beyond the true "faith," whilst the Ottomans gained a superficial and uncertain grip on isolated urban centres of this remote imperial outpost.

With the search and exploitation of oil resources the new intruders were only allowed on sufferance to enter this empty and unfriendly land. Regarded as "infidels" and with suspicion, whose very presence polluted the holy soil, they were prevented from any move that might be interpreted as "ownership" or the colonisation of the desert land. By this means the great Sheikhs or Kings or Emirs of the Arabian peninsula quickly accrued huge wealth through the skills and labour of their Western visitors, but this was not reciprocated by any sense of gratitude towards those who had brought them the riches of Croesus. On the contrary, their presence ensured segregation and confinement to compounds and this distance exacerbated the fear and loathing of the foreign culture. If there was a sense of gratitude – and there was – it was to God alone, who was responsible for transforming and enriching the lives of the Arab people through the gift of oil. Oil, therefore, was not seen as an accidental fact of existence, but as God's intentional gift for the purpose of justly rewarding his faithful and deeply religious adherents.

There was, however, another and more significant force that transformed the Islamic culture of the Arabian peninsula. In the 18th century the powerful preacher, Muhammad ibn Abd al-Wahab, launched a campaign against what he saw as the lax tendencies of contemporary Islam with the accretions and corruption that had developed in the medicval period. He called for the purification of the Sunni sect and a return to the earliest doctrines and practices of Islam as embodied in the Koran and the Sunna. With the support of the neighbouring prince, Muhammad ibn Saud, Wahabism expanded over the next two and a half centuries to dominate most the peninsula, initially to confront Ottoman power based in Constantinople, and subsequently, as a militant religion aspiring to worldwide dominion.

It is impossible to over-emphasise the significance of Wahabism as the most powerful political-religious movement of our time. Its religious emotive force dwarfs the political power of Marxism and its opposing ideology Neo-Liberalism, as they have existed until the very recent past. The power of Islam as a threat to the advanced industrial economies has seemed to put the old left/right divide into the shade, and it is that divide that has dominated and split society over the past two centuries. New conflictual patterns are emerging that were unimaginable until yesterday. The intensity of these forces becomes most apparent on recollecting that few Marxists have turned themselves into living bombs and none amongst the Neo-Liberals.

It is difficult for those in the industrialised world to comprehend what seems the irrationality of such an ideology as Islamic fundamentalism seizing ultimate control. In this respect, only one comparison comes easily to mind, viz., the takeover of the Roman Empire by Christianity in the 4th century AD. In the eyes of the majority, for a period of 300 years, Christianity was regarded as an eccentric, intolerant and life-denying ideology on account of its hatred of classical values, art, and literature of the Romano-Hellenic civilisation. This hatred is most clearly expressed in the last book of the *New Testament*, being the book of *Revelation*. Early Christianity was driven by an underclass that was averse to reason and the accepted values of the time, and on those rare occasions when its adherents were subjected to persecution, torture, or death, there were few who came to their defence.

For a period of 200 years, the educated classes, and the greatest thinkers of the time (such as the Stoics) held them in askance. By the year 300 AD it was still considered unlikely that Christianity should take over the political control of the classical world. But by the year 330 AD the Roman Empire was firmly under the grip of Christian authority. Whilst the establishment of Christianity culminated in bringing a better moral environment to the civilised world, it was achieved through the sacrifice of free thought and the universal toleration of religious beliefs and practices. However, this better moral environment was not extended to the abolition or slavery or the security of political rights for the individual. As the church strengthened as an organised power in league with a feudal military elite, it eventually mutated into a tyrannical and corrupt authority that was not effectively challenged for 1,200 years, i.e. with the Reformation early in the 16th century.

In the light of the circumstances surrounding the sudden and unanticipated emergence of Christianity in the 4th century, it is not entirely inconceivable that Islam might likewise seize control of the Western world, i.e., the North American continent and the Euro-Caucasian landmass before the close of the 21st century. There are other sinister comparisons between Christianity's seizure of power in the 4th century and the distinct possibility of Islam's seizure of power in the 21st century.

By the 4th century AD the birth rate of the ethnic Romano-Hellenic peoples of the central Empire had already collapsed generations beforehand.   In the 1st century the Emperor Augustus had called for the strengthening of marriage and the encouragement of childbearing. At the present day the birth rate of Caucasian peoples across the entire Euro-Asian and North American landmasses and island outposts has crashed. So, too, has the birth rate of the Confucian peoples of China, Korea, and Japan – and so the comparison extends well beyond the racial dimension. In ancient Rome as in the modern world it is the most educated, innovative, creative, and cultured sectors of the population that have chosen not to reproduce themselves in maintaining the values of their civilisation.

Another significant comparison is the collapse of productivity in the Italian mainland by the 4th century. This began with the loss of smallholdings granted to the military after a lifetime of service. Eventually, due to the accumulation of property into ever fewer hands, those smallholders were dispossessed by a wealthy financial elite. Ever larger estates were then worked by the lesser efficiency of slave labour. Increasingly food production became dependent on imports from the fertile soil of North Africa and Egypt. In the 21st century both Europe and America have become dependent for most of their manufactured and industrial goods on the Far East, giving rise to a self-destructive economy dependent on usury and debts that can never be paid.

The last comparison to be made is the arrival of huge migrant populations. Over a period of centuries the Romano-Hellenic order was swamped with barbarian hordes at odds with the civilised rational values of the classical world. This initially occurred through the arrival of slaves, being the captives of occupied territories, and as soon as they had been manumitted, they chose to remain in the Italian mainland in enjoying the material benefits and security of a higher civilisation, so contributing to a higher birth rate than that of the ethnic population.

Meanwhile, the policy of extending Roman citizenship to those from distant territories encouraged the settlement of those introducing cults and superstitions clearly conflicting with the tradition of logical thinking, or commitment to constructive reason in building a better future. Leading historians have cited the rule of such foreign-inspired emperors, as Elagabalus as the most striking symptoms of cultural decline. The frequent invasions and occupation of the Italian mainland completes the picture of this sorry story, for Romano-Hellenic civilisation was virtually destroyed even though the ruling authorities may have remained in denial of a fact too painful to recognise as actuality. In the 21st century, the possibility of the migration of millions to Western Europe, with their higher birth rate confronting ethnic peoples with a low birth rate would lead inevitably to the collapse of the so-called "West" and all the cultural and ethical values it had cherished and defended for so long through times of war and peace.

In returning to the question of Wahabism, which ideologically is the greatest threat to our contemporary technological civilisation it should be noted that oil revenues alone have lit the spark enabling the worldwide spread of that particular form of Islamic fundamentalism.

The Kingdom of Saudi Arabia, and in its wake, the smaller Gulf States have invested billions of dollars worldwide in propagating the Islamic message. In Britain alone, for example, the Gulf States contributed £233.5m between 1995 and 2008 to the following seven universities for Islamic studies: Oxford, Cambridge, the UCL, the LSE, Exeter, Dundee, and the City University London.

In addition, the late King Fahad of Saudi Arabia contributed £75m to the Oxford Centre for Islamic Studies, and one of his nephews, Prince Alwaleed bin Talal, gave £8m to Cambridge and Edinburgh; and the LSE's Centre for Middle Eastern Studies received £9m from the UAE. Whilst these substantial funds have been contributed under the guise of, "promoting greater understanding of Islam," the recent research of Prof. Anthony Glees has concluded that their real agenda is to push an extreme ideology and act as a form of propaganda for Wahabism in British universities. They promote, he argues, "the wrong sort of education by the wrong set of people, funded by the wrong sorts of donor."[2] But the above contributions represent a small fraction of the huge sums distributed throughout the wider world in the cause of Islam.

A more sinister development than the propagation of Islamic fundamentalism by Arab States is that Wahabism has taken off as a power in its own right under its own terms. This has led to the ironic situation whereby it has rebounded on Saudi Arabia and other Gulf States that have found themselves in conflict with various offshoots of their own religious ideology. The Mujahideen of the 1980s and 90s in Afghanistan was initially financed by the US and the Saudis in the war to drive out Soviet forces occupying that country.

The movement – or a great part of it – was subsequently re-organised and financed by Osama bin Laden, and after it splintered into conflicting groups, there emerged the Taliban, a Pakistani promoted organisation. The Taliban comprised those who had grown up in Pakistan refugee camps where they were taught in Saudi-backed Wahabi madrassas. Within several years, these and other organisations as Al-Qaeda, Boko Haram, Al-Shabaab, and later Isis or Daesh, all found themselves in opposition to the Kingdom of Saudi Arabia and other Gulf States.

Consequently, although the Kingdom and her close Gulf neighbours are seen as a moderate influence in Middle East politics, she is currently additionally in conflict with Shia forces in Yemen to her south east and Iran to the north west, as well as with a perceived heretical Shia sect, the Alawites, controlling Syria under the rule of Basher al-Assad; in addition to opposition from various Wahabi-influenced terrorist forces cited

---

[2] See Stephen Pollard's article, "Are our universities selling themselves to the highest bidder,?" *Daily Telegraph*, 4th March 2011.

above. All this illustrates the entangled and chaotic nature of Middle East politics that is difficult to disentangle from religious differences that compound the intensity of an uncompromising hatred and determination to pursue narrow local interests to the death.

Islam, or for that matter, any social organisation can only be properly or objectively understood within a sociological context. This means that no organisation can be properly understood through its own definition or perception of itself. All organisations invent their own rationale or justification for existence that may differ from the true reality. Social organisations come into existence through circumstances beyond their own control or comprehension.

They are little more that the instruments or victims of their time, but if they aspire to broadening their influence or gaining power in the community, they must invent a mythology or an attractive ideology in gaining followers. Muslims claim that theirs is a religion of peace, for Islam is translated as "peace," to "resign oneself," or "submission." But others outside the faith may have a different or more objective rendering of this interpretation. They may interpret this "peace" as the peace of death. After all, "resignation" or "submission" equals a negative rather than a positive stance. The Muslim will of course reply that "submission to God" cannot possibly be interpreted in a negative sense, but then the question arises as to the definition of God.

In the modern world the definition of God is better achieved by philosophers rather by theologians, i.e., by a Spinoza, a Kant, or a Locke, or by those early 18th century English Deists, most of whom were in Holy orders, but because of their love of reason, tended more towards philosophical than theological thought. As soon as such an intellectual approach is formulated, and rationality is substituted for revelation, it is then possible to connect the conception of God to the real world and then to the facts of psychology. Only then is it possible to discuss religion and God in a meaningful sense, and avoid muddled thinking or what might be described as the expression of "nonsense."

The problem of Islamic fundamentalism – or the dominating form of Islam now threatening the rest of the world – is that it is incompatible with modern civilisation in every conceivable sense. This means that the two cannot coexist together for the longer term. The time must come when the one must destroy the other, or sensible compromise for long-term stability must be achieved. The incompatibility of Islam in every day situations in an advanced industrial society is most clearly demonstrated through the frequent demands of its religious practices in interrupting the busy schedules of ordinary life to an intolerable degree.

The five times daily call to prayer, and each day at a different time set according to the phases of sunrise and sunset, may not be a burden on the mind of the desert dweller, but it most certainly is on the majority of the industrial world's busy population. The first call to prayer at approximately 4.30 am entails sleep deprivation for many — especially for those approaching the later years of life – and hence is disadvantageous to good health. Those calls to prayer during the daylight hours entail a major nuisance in adversely affecting the course of business when important negotiations are suddenly broken off for twenty or thirty minutes with the excuse that a visit must be made to the mosque.

There are other much more serious situations, of course, as when operatives of complex machinery, or drivers of vehicles on land, sea, or air may put others at risk in addition to themselves. The law of illegal seclusion, meanwhile, produces so many difficulties in conducting ordinary life in a modern society that complicated and expensive means must be found in resolving the situation. When it comes to staffing the crews of Saudi Airways, for example, an impossible situation is reached as IATA insists on mixed gender crews, and so non-Muslim foreigners of several nationalities need to be employed.

All this has an influence on the employment patterns of Muslims abiding by the stricter rules of the faith, so that highly technological occupations tend to be avoided in favour of more traditional careers as buying and selling. Arabia has always been a major artery of trade. The resolution between the obstruction of ancient practices and the demands of modernity is something that can only be properly attended to within the Islamic faith.

Arabs and others supporting radical Islam are perfectly content to take every advantage of our technological civilisation, but they are not prepared to tolerate those conditions that enable an advanced industrial society to flourish and exist. That is, our civilisation could not develop further and take a step into the future unless an absolute freedom of thought is guaranteed to the individual in enabling inventiveness and creativity. It is impossible for a Newton or an Einstein to emerge in a vacuum, for they could only have come into being in highly sophisticated and educated societies that allowed their ideas to be freely tested and discussed. And such societies are only possible when the fullest freedom is granted to both ideas and people howsoever eccentric, outrageous, mediocre or inspired, ridiculous, or downright malicious they happen to be. A substantial middle class and moderate affluence is certainly a minimum requirement for such a society.

It is perhaps a significant but ironic fact that the solemn and puritanical period of the English Commonwealth (1649-1660) was a desert in terms of inventiveness and creativity, but as soon as the good-natured Merry Monarch (who personally engaged in scientific research) ascended the throne with all his pleasure-seeking and immorality, the country shot ahead in terms of scientific invention, superb architecture, the theatre, music, and the other arts. Even some of the greatest Puritan works of literature were written and published in the Restoration period, e.g., Milton's *Paradise Lost* (1664) and Bunyan's *Pilgrim's Progress* (1678). Both Newton and Einstein were religious in their own idiosyncratic ways, but had they been born in another epoch, they might have been burned at the stake for daring to express heretical views.

The contemporary Arab lives in a strangely anachronistic society. In the morning he may use an electric toothbrush or prepare himself a smoothy in a Kenwood mixer, and at noon on a Friday he may witness the stoning to death of an adulteress after prayers in the mosque, or more often, the beheading of several men for homosexual practices. If he finds himself in a room with a woman who is not a close relative, he exposes himself to the criminal charge of "illegal seclusion," and by the same law, no workplace can employ men and women together. In ensuring segregation at such joyous events as wedding receptions, the latter are held in different hotels for men and women, the bride and groom usually being enthroned at the women's reception.

Whilst Saudi Arabia provides separate beaches for *Celibates*, i.e., for men and *Families*, i.e., for bona fide married couples with children, there are none for women only, for the latter are only allowed to wander from their homes in the company of close relatives or appointed guardians. Likewise, there is no seating for women on Saudi busses, where they are confined to standing room only in segregated compartments at the back of vehicles. I have seen women fighting and tearing at one another's clothing to cram into the back of a crowded bus, whilst the seated front part of the vehicle for male passengers, remained almost empty.

In the women's university male lecturers can only communicate with their students via an intercom and TV screen in the lecture hall. In Arabia one needs to move easily from the 6th century to the 21st century, and then back again without any sense of the abnormal. Whilst the Arab enjoys a high standard of living with every Western manufactured convenience, on the other hand, he presents the image of an irresponsible child incapable of appreciating or even understanding the causes for his exceptionally good fortune to live in a world that is 1,400 years ahead of his nurtured mindset.

The Arab could enjoy none of the advanced technological benefits on which he is dependent if it was not for the freedom and free societies enabling such advances to be made. A censored freedom is either no freedom or so crippling as to restrict innovation and change. Freedom demands neutrality in terms of good or bad, the desirable or undesirable, and cannot be shackled by custom or prejudice. The speculative mind knows no frontiers whither it will go in the search for truth and progress.

CHAPTER 2
Europe's Age of Religious Shame

"Men never do evil so completely and cheerfully as when they
do it from religious conviction."
Blaise Pascal, *Pensées*, Sec. xiv, No. 895.

If the non-Islamic world is apparently so much in advance of
those who are described as "infidels," it is necessary to
search for the reasons why. There is nothing intrinsically
good or virtuous about Western people – or those further afield.
They are neither more nor less fallible than their Islamic
brothers and sisters, but the circumstances of history have
perhaps made them, not as individuals, but as socially
interacting beings or groups, a better, broader-minded and more
humane people. There was a time when Europeans were as
savage – or more so – than those amongst the worst elements of
the Taliban or Isis of today.

If the beginning of the age for the struggle for freedom,
i.e., the Reformation early in the 16th century, did not bring out
the best in human nature it certainly brought out the worst. And
what puts an even darker light on the matter is that these men
were supposedly seeking the truth through their service to God.
The Catholic Church had indeed become corrupt through
luxury, simony, and a variety of vices more common to human
nature. The Protestants were justified in raising their flag of
revolt, and initially they concentrated on their true grounds of
complaint, viz., the sale of indulgences enabling an easier entry
into heaven. This was the first great insurance scam in the
history of the West, and it was promoted by an army of hard
headed salesmen.

But once a long-established institution comes under attack,
other faults are soon uncovered, and through a process of
splintering and quarrelling groups, chaos follows in its wake.
History has tended to cover up the failings and even the
criminality of the leading lights of the Reformation, e.g.,
Luther's call on the nobles to put down the peasants, who had

risen in revolt, like "mad dogs;" or his pamphlet, *On The Jews and their Lies*, where he calls for the destruction of their homes and synagogues, and the confiscation of their money and the curtailment of their freedom.

This piece of writing is more reminiscent of the obscenities of Julius Streicher's Nazi articles in *Der Stürmer*, than that of a man of the cloth. These unpleasant facts have been buried in the past, and the contemporary German Lutheran church is possibly amongst the most enlightened and humane of any religious organisation on our planet. For over a hundred years the University of Tübingen, for example, has played a leading part in promoting Lutheran thought in attempting to update the doctrines and beliefs of Christianity. But the past nonetheless remains a blot on history.

Meanwhile, the founder of the Reformed Church, Jean Calvin, was hardly less guilty of malicious crimes than his archrival, Luther. Calvin's most wicked deed was the part he played in the murder of Michael Servetus. The latter was not only a truth-seeking Spanish theological scholar and the founder of Unitarian thought, but a scientist and polymath who was the first to correctly describe the function of pulmonary circulation. He entered into a disputatious correspondence with Calvin, and through an intricate deceit was persuaded to meet the great Reformer in his lair in Geneva.

As Servetus would have been a foreigner in the Canton of Geneva, he should have been legally protected from any harm through the expression of his opinions beyond an order for his deportation. Unfortunately, almost as soon as he arrived in the city, the law was circumvented and through the authority of Calvin, in conjunction with the Genevan Council of Twenty-Five, he was arrested, tried and found guilty on two counts: firstly, of Non-Trinitarianism; and secondly, of Anti-infant baptism. He was then condemned to be burnt alive atop a pyre of his own books, and Calvin expressed the wish that green wood be used as a fuel to prolong his agony. This execution was carried out on 27th October 1553.

There was a mutual hatred between Calvin and Luther, as indeed there was amongst most the leaders of breakaway groups claiming the incontrovertible truth, and struggling for the absolute control of society in opposition to any alternative ways of thinking. It is worth noting what marked the main differences between these leading religious movements. Whilst Calvinism is most distinguished through Predestination, or the idea that God predestines some people to be saved whilst others are condemned to hell, irrespective of the strivings of the individual for salvation; Lutheranism is based on the idea of justification through faith alone; whilst Catholicism is based on good works and the fulfilment of established rites.

These are no more than crude and thumbnail descriptions of the leading Christian churches, but as soon as deeper attempts are made to understand their theologies, they become evermore abstruse or metaphysical. This is because they present concepts that are impossible to prove through a commonsense approach to existence: e.g., the Trinity, the Virgin Birth, or Revelation, i.e., the disclosure of knowledge through a divine or supernatural agency.

There are only two ways to accept facts, or to ascertain the truth of opinions: either through reason which may be clearly demonstrated; or through mysticism, which is the choice to believe in an object or idea because it is perceived as imperative to do so on moral grounds without the need for a rational explanation. And this is the sole cause for the bloodshed and atrocities that have marked the history of religion over the ages. No man has killed another because he asserted that two and two made five. He has merely been laughed at and dismissed as a lunatic. But religion is rarely a laughing matter.

Heresy, or a slight slip-up in misconstruing the correct definition of a complex theological dogma may easily lead to the death penalty. Why is this? It is because commonsense assertions, such as two and two make four, or that day follows night, have no emotive power. Their acceptance is universal and incontrovertible. But the assertion of the Virgin Birth, or the truth of the Trinity, are so definitive and demanding, that their denial is taken as an outrage. It is because these concepts are so abstruse and contradict commonsense, or amount to nonsense in the everyday world, that they arouse such strong emotions.

Theologians who remain locked away in their cells for years developing their nebulous metaphysical structures through lengthy dissertations are quite naturally put into a rage if anyone questions the truth of their conclusions. Luther and Calvin, and dozens of their like, spent a lifetime filling reams of paper, and if their writings are repudiated by those who fail to comprehend their ideas, then abuse and vitriol is their only outlet if the pathos of sweet reason is closed to their mode of explication.

The Reformation and the Counter-Reformation, and the growth of new religions and sects throughout central and Western Europe were the precursor of far worse to come. The early 16th century marked the emergence of new religious ideas whilst the later 16th and first half of the 17th centuries marked the politicisation of these ideas within the nation state. When this stage is reached religion is used unknowingly as a weapon for fighting causes which have little or nothing to do with religion, such as re-establishing the balance of power between competing states; the settlement of dynastic disputes; resorting to the conquest of fertile land, or *Lebensraum*, in the event of over-population; or conflicts between different nationalities or cultural or language groups, for any number of questionable reasons, etc. In these situations religion is always a useful tool in stimulating hatred or the efforts of war, for the God of one's enemy is never quite as virtuous or as justifiable as the God of one's own country.

In the latter part of the 16th century, and particularly during the Thirty Years War (1618-1648), Europe may be said to have passed through her "Syria-like" episode of all against all. During this period there was an acceleration of senseless bloodshed, such as the St. Bartholomew massacre in France, when thousands of Huguenots were dragged from their houses and slaughtered irrespective of age or sex; or when Spanish troops wiped-out entire populations in villages and towns in the southern Netherlands, amongst other atrocities.

The crescendo of this wickedness was reached during the Thirty Years War when Germany was reduced to a parched wilderness of ashes and ruin at the hands of foreign invaders, for which she needed more than a century to recover. This war was supposedly a conflict between Protestants and Catholics, but the complex reality of the situation puts it in a very different light. For example, whilst Cardinal Richelieu, the chief minister of France, was crushing Protestants in his own country, in Germany he was cynically supporting the Protestant cause in containing the threatening power of the Austrian Habsburgs. Whilst the surrounding powers were devastating Germany from all directions, it may be observed that many mercenary Protestant troops, even generals, were fighting for the Imperial Catholic cause, and vice versa, Catholics were drawing the sword on behalf of Protestantism. But mercenary troops have always served those who offered the highest rewards, and are rarely drawn by the appeals of ideology or the rightness of a cause.

In England, meanwhile, ever-apprehensive, but protected by the stormy waters of her sea-girt coast, from the reign of Elizabeth to that of James II, Catholics were perceived (and often were) the Al-Qaeda of their age. One assassination plot and conspiracy followed by another followed in quick succession, the most notorious being the Gunpowder Plot of 1605 to kill the King and members of both Houses of Parliament ignited by a single spark, and it is no wonder that government was forced into the extreme measure of passing the death penalty on priests or persons secretly attempting to hold the Catholic mass or illegally entering the country. Panic and ruthlessness was the inevitable consequence of horrific terrorism, fear for the loss of freedom, and the morbid anxiety that springs from an invisible enemy.

The worst of the anti-Catholic paranoia in England was brought to an end through the notorious episode of the so-called Popish Plot of 1678-81. This fictitious conspiracy to murder Charles II culminated in the execution of at least twenty-two persons in addition to the arrest, trial, persecution and imprisonment of many more, including prominent nobles and other personalities – Samuel Pepys being amongst their number. One of the measures taken was the expulsion of Catholics from London who were forbidden to come within ten miles of the capital.

The conspiracy was generated by a notorious de-frocked clergyman, Titus Oates, who had alternated his adherence between the Baptists and the Church of England, had travelled on the Continent, served on several ships, and was dropped from a charge of buggery on account of his status as a man in "Holy Orders." It was at the time of his pretended conversion to Catholicism to spy on the Jesuits that he decided on his mischievous scheme to stir up hysteria against that faith, together with Israel Tonge, a fanatically anti-Catholic clergyman, believed by many to be insane. When false accusations and affidavits of conspiracy to murder were presented to the King, he contemptuously dismissed them as absurd. It was only when these inventions were presented to the government that Parliament decided on serious measures.

It was then that accusations followed thick and fast, becoming evermore incredible. Eventually the King's brother, the Duke of York, a recent Catholic convert, was implicated in the conspiracy, an absurdity in view of the warm relationship between the brothers; and worst of all, the Queen consort, Catherine of Braganza, was accused of scheming with her physician for the murder of her husband, and detailed accounts of the rooms and persons in Somerset House were presented as proof of guilt. The King at once recognised the falsity of the cleverly assembled evidence, and was outraged by attempts to blacken the reputation of his virtuous consort whom he had so ill-used in the past. The outcome of this dismal episode to persecute a religious minority was that Oates was eventually charged with perjury for which was flogged and imprisoned for a 3-year period.

The Peace of Westphalia in 1648, which brought about the end of the Thirty Years War, was the great turning point in European history. Although religious forces were still to exert a background influence amongst the great powers, and discriminatory social legislation within nation states continued to be introduced and applied, there were to be no more religious wars. A feeling of disgust at what had occurred during the recent past drove ahead the need for secularism and the will for freedom and new thinking.

Protestantism had broken certain bonds restricting the free interpretation of the sacred book, but such freedom had been cancelled out by a destructive conflict imposing new restrictions replacing those that had been overcome. Religion alone, or in itself, did not bring the freedom that humankind desired. Something more was called for. A new rationalism, or approach to reason, was the only path to resolving the problems of humanity. The horrors of the past drove intellectual leaders and the collective consciousness of ordinary thinking people towards an age of science, inventiveness, and peaceful contemplation for a better future, in the second half of the 17th century. These tendencies extended to art and literature, and the reform of manners, and to a world that was a more civilised place than heretofore.

CHAPTER 3
The Purification of Religion through Rationality

"I must ever believe that religion substantially good which produces an honest life, and we have been authorised by one whom you and I equally respect, to judge of the tree by its fruit."

Thomas Jefferson, *Writings*, Vol. XIV, p. 197.

A healthy reaction against religiosity or the tendency to mysticism was not only a natural but an inevitable response for well-meaning people in view of those past events as recorded in the previous chapter. With the Enlightenment at the start of the 18th century, the accusation of *Enthusiasm* was thrown at those who caught the religious "bug."

The Enthusiast was held in either ridicule or contempt throughout the 18th century. This did not mean that the church withheld from good works. Quite the contrary! The eminent historian, Sir George Clark, has interestingly observed that, "the religious life in the reigns of William III and Anne was better than its ecclesiastical history. It did not produce a single martyr, not a saint, nor a devotional classic; but it was fruitful in all those charitable and humane activities which are the religious aspect of English practical sense. The forces which were bringing into being the great humanitarian movement of the 18th century were deeper and wider than the disputes of sects, as wide as the desire for reasonableness which was appeasing the wranglings about creeds."[3]

On the same theme, another Oxford historian, Basil Williams, has written about "the lethargy and want of spirituality" of the English church at the time, noting that "by a strange paradox, though the workaday religion preached and practised by the mass of the clergy, both established and dissenting, has rarely been so uninspiring as in this century, yet few ages in our history have been so prolific in serious thought

---

[3] *The Later Stuarts 1660-1714*, OUP, 2nd ed., 1956, p. 157.

about the fundamentals and justification of the whole scheme of Christianity."[4] One of the greatest religious thinkers of the day, and a prolific writer, was Joseph Butler, Bishop of Durham, and it is interesting to note his testy response to the approach of the *enthusiast*, John Wesley, whom he put firmly in his place with the words, "Sir, the pretending to extraordinary revelations and gifts of the Holy Ghost is a horrid thing, a very horrid thing."[5] This illustrates the altercation that may arise when Fanatical and Reasoning minds are confronted by an uncompromising situation.

The age of Reason, which heralded the Enlightenment saw the production of many books that questioned established theology or the realm over which it might extend. Most notably was Pierre Bayle's massive encyclopaedia of philosophical and religious scepticism, the *Dictionaire historique et critique*, which for safety reason was first published in the Netherlands in 1697, and two years previously, the founder of Liberal thought in terms of toleration, John Locke, had published his *Reasonableness of Christianity as delivered in the Scriptures.*

But long before that Sir Francis Bacon had argued that a complete separation should be respected between "divine and humane learning," and that neither should encroach on the authority of the other. These arguments were presented in a circumspect book, *The Advancement of Learning* (1605) dedicated respectfully to the King. In the middle of the 17th century Thomas Hobbes produced his great political work, *Leviathan* (1651), based on his study of human psychology, and the relationship of humankind with authority and the emergence of the state, rather than on the more traditional approach of turning to the generally accepted explanations of Biblical texts. When he did resort to quoting religious script he was deferring to the prejudices of the time, but this was not sufficient to exempt him from accusations of atheism.

The most significant development of the time with regard to the transformation of religious attitudes was the emergence of

---

[4] *The Whig Supremacy 1714-1760*, OUP, 2nd ed., 1960, p. 83.
[5] Ibid., quoted p. 90.

Deism, most prominently during the first half of the 18th century. Deism was concerned with the core purpose of religion, i.e., with the nature of God, and it is to the everlasting glory of English intellectual life that we produced so many leading Deists during this period whose influence was extended far and wide on the European mainland and eventually to America. Most Deists were men already in Holy orders, and their truth-seeking task was to define a belief in God that was stripped of theological prejudice, and all the superstition and what might be interpreted as "nonsense" that had enslaved humanity for centuries.

Deism entails a deeply serious approach to the nature and existence of God, if indeed He is to be made a subject of belief. If the majority – or too many – reject the existence of God, or cannot adhere to His belief, then there is something seriously awry in the arguments for His reality. It is not that disbelievers should be dismissed, or held in the wrong, but the arguments with which they are presented. If God is to be understood as a serious concept, then it is only right and respectful to His being that He is described in rational terms acceptable to the commonsense reasoning of the ordinary person.

Demand in the belief in Revelation is not only insulting to the intelligence of the individual, but more significantly, insulting to the existence of God in denying his belief to so many. Furthermore, the psychological implications of Revelation (or belief in a supernatural agency) is grossly immoral on two counts: firstly, because it appeals to irrationality, or what cannot be proven as true; and secondly, because it is aroused by a nervous or disordered excitation of the brain, often drug-induced.

In illustrating this situation, it is unnecessary to turn to the fumes arising from the rocks at Delphi in throwing the Pythoness into a trance in predicting future events. One may turn to the notorious Leyden jar and electrical shock treatments applied by John Wesley to prospective converts to the faith, or the ruthlessness and contemporary trickery used at the present day by many American evangelical churches in arousing converts to a state of hysteria in demonstrating the convictions of their "true faith." These, of course, are extreme examples, but they display the measures that may be taken in overriding the purpose of Revelation or the demands of reason.

Irrationality is immoral as it too easily facilitates evil of every kind. That is not to suggest that rationality also is not incapable of producing evil, but it is a better path in ensuring the good life. Belief in the Deity, therefore, should be based on the judgement of the cool mind in seeking to avoid the excitation of the nervous system.

Most 18th century Deists sought to work with circumspection so as not to offend the sensibilities of the more religious in their midst, but some over-stepped the mark, and even in that tolerant age, when libel and blasphemy seemed almost beyond the law, they were imprisoned for their offence against society. The leading overtly acknowledged Deists of this period (for there were many others following a similar line of thought), may be cited, Ralph Cudworth; Charles Blount; John Toland; Thomas Woolston; Anthony Collins; William Wallaston; Matthew Tindal; Thomas Chubb; Thomas Morgan; Lord Bolingbroke, and Peter Annet. Lastly, it would be amiss to fail noting the name of Lord Herbert of Cherbury (1583-1648), regarded as the founding proponent of Deism (although he never used the term) for his book, *On Truth, as it is distinguished from Revelation, the Probable, the Possible, and the False*, first published in Paris in 1624 and subsequently in London in 1633 and 1645, that went straight to the root of the problematical deceit of conventional religious teaching.

In the early 18th century French translations of the English Deists were often printed in the Netherlands and smuggled into their destined country where they were read with eagerness by the intelligentsia. Voltaire, who spent two years in England, where he became an ardent anglophile, was amongst the first to promote the Deist cause. In his campaign against the oppression and unspeakable cruelties of the Catholic Church (such as breaking on the wheel), he closely analysed the Bible and its teachings and reduced them to ridicule and contempt in the eyes of right-thinking people who upheld the principles of justice and humanity. Although Voltaire was falsely accused of atheism, he was the man who boldly proclaimed "that if there was no God it would ne necessary to invent him."

Nonetheless, Deism in France had the misfortune to mutate into atheism, not because of the innate proclivities of French thought but because of the total corruption of the French church that brought such hatred upon its head. Whilst the English church was able to bend with the wind of modernism, the French church was torn up by its roots. This is not to suggest that the French church should be identified with Catholicism as part of a wider European movement. Since the Counter-Reformation the papacy and the broader church had undergone many reforms, and much corruption which had instigated Protestantism had long since been cleansed. The popes of the 18th century did not follow the pattern of those who had preceded them in earlier centuries, and in 1740 one of the greatest popes of the modern age was to ascend the throne, viz., Benedict XIV, who was to reign for 18 years.

This pope, who had been known as Prospero Lorenzo Lambertini, was intelligent, understanding of the needs of the time, with a renowned sense of humour, and was loved by the ordinary people of the Papal States. Amongst his many reforms in improving the training of the priesthood, and in purifying the thinking and practices of the church, he is perhaps best remembered for two Bulls in accommodating non-Christian words and usages to express Christian ideas and practices of native cultures, initiatives that had first been embarked upon by the Jesuit Order in their Indian and Chinese missions. This gesture of multi-culturalism was a major contribution in uniting the world towards a greater understanding. It is perhaps remarkable that Voltaire, who had been a scourge of the church, entered into a friendly correspondence with Benedict, respecting him for his mild disposition and conciliatory attitude in peacefully settling matters of dispute, the two enjoying mutual respect. This is a notable example of when the potential for enmity may be turned into respectful understanding through the virtue of the stronger or more authoritative party.

Whilst Deism in France mutated into open atheism, in America it tended to morph into Unitarianism by the start of the 19th century. To understand these contrasts, it should be borne in mind that whilst Deism entered France to be used as an attack on the established church, in America it was welcomed as an instrument of reason in constructing a better material world. Tom Paine's, *The Age of Reason*, was perhaps the greatest Deist tract to be published in America. Many of the leading Founding fathers were unapologetic Deists, and they felt this in no way conflicted with their Christian principles or with the various churches to which they belonged.

Deism was also a significant intellectual influence in Prussia, and Frederick the Great (that sometime friend of Voltaire) ordered the translation of those English tracts that had not already reached the German public. Prussia had already welcomed the religiously persecuted of the world, viz., the expelled Huguenots of France, with all their skills and knowledge, and Jews from the four quarters of Europe. As a practical man with mild religious feelings he declared, "that everyone should go to heaven in the way he chooses." His religious liberalism was perhaps most clearly marked by the fact that Berlin was the only capital in Protestant Europe that authorised the building of a Catholic cathedral (St. Hedwig's) in a world still reflecting religious divisions through the denomination of its ruling princes.

Those who may hold in disdain the Deism or nature of religiosity in the England of the 18th century should bear the following in mind: as a percentage of publications produced, more volumes of sermons were produced in that century than in any other in recorded history. Furthermore, in regard to a secular approach to morals or ethics, more works were published during that period than at any other time, not only in such media as leading literary journals as the *Spectator, Tatler, Guardian, Rambler, Idler,* etc., but also in the form of digressional essays in leading novels of the period. This demonstrates clearly the seriousness with which leading thinkers throughout the Enlightenment were obsessed by questions of right and wrong, and their invaluable contribution as a heritage for our own time.

Whilst the 19th century experienced a religious retrogression towards the spirituality of the medieval era, both through the evangelistic teachings of non-conformist sects and the contrasting direction of the established Church – the latter particularly through the Oxford movement with the absurdity of its return to Gothic practices and architecture – a more enlightened approach to modernising religion nonetheless continued to advance. This was achieved through the more scientific and critical developments of the age, particularly as led by Germany. Immanuel Kant had already produced his *Religion Within The Limits of Reason Alone* in 1793, a sufficiently provocative work to be suppressed by the narrow-minded nephew and successor of Frederick the Great, Frederick William II, and much later by such diverse dictators as Generalissimo Franco in Spain, and Joseph Stalin in Soviet Russia.

The wars and resentments of conflicting orthodoxies were now long forgotten by the educated elite, and truth-seeking critical thought could now be pursued with cool heads, undisturbed by controversy in an objective environment. One of the leading books of the new century was David Friedrich Strauss's monumental *Life of Jesus* (1836), translated by George Eliot – a work that confirmed her existing agnosticism.

Perhaps the most interesting and valuable work later in the century was Ernest Renan's 8-volume *History of The Origins of Christianity* (1863-81), which through its profound scholarship, examined all the surrounding psychological circumstances of the movement. Innumerable books have followed until the present day, many written by churchmen and churchwomen, who chose to question age-old beliefs or present them within a more realistic context. The purpose of these writings has been to purify religion, or strengthen its credibility as the acceptance of truth in a highly complex technological world that has become impatient or intolerant of assertions defying practical demonstration.

In addition to the clash of political interests and the development of intellectual thought in advancing changes to religious belief, the greatest influence in modern times towards agnosticism has been the consequences of science – particularly the benefits of medicine. The strongest power drawing men and women to religion is helplessness or desperation in the face of inescapable misfortune, perhaps most commonly the loss of children or frequent outbreaks of contagious fatal diseases. Medicine has removed both these dangers, and at the present time it is usually only the diseases of old age that are unable to confront the threat of death, and that occurs when the inevitable is close by.

From the closing decades of the 19th century an overweening self-assurance seized the public mood and religion was declared as the out-dated superstition of the past as humankind took over his own fate without the need for a higher power. But hubris followed in the wake of Nietzsche's boast that "God is dead," for war, natural disasters, and the foolishness of humankind in the government of society, unexpectedly brought unimaginable disorder and misery in the 20th century. We should now be sufficiently percipient to realise that God is as essential to our own age as in any other, for there remain spheres of life over which the individual has no control, or the experience of misfortunes that are irreversible. The only question remaining is to correctly define the nature of that God.

The changes in the intellectual environment over the past 300 years have clearly been to place the leading Christian and other churches in a quandary. This is because of the doubt in which their beliefs are placed: is the church to stand by the literal interpretation of established dogma as held by the ignorant and usually unbelieving majority, in the hope that either blind faith or ignorance will ultimately save the church; or is the church to stand by a modern, poetic, or symbolical interpretation of ancient dogmas with the risk of losing the few remaining faithful? These conflicting choices are made in the light of the fact that many educated clergyman- and women hold theological principles quite different or more complex than those they are prepared to deliver from the pulpit. The intellectual ambience of our seminaries is quite different from that found amongst our pews. Consequently, most clergy are fearful of addling the minds of their congregations.

The truth of the situation, however, is even more complex than this. I do not believe that most clergy have a proper understanding of the mindset of their congregations. Whilst it may be suggested that the clergy adopt a hypocritical stance towards their congregations in deferring to their simplistic grasp of important principles, even going so far as to flatter their infantilism; I believe that congregations in their turn exert an even grosser hypocrisy in misleading their church leaders as to their own thought processes. The relationship between the clergy and their flock has, of course, for centuries always been ambiguous and sometimes a subject for humour and secret sniggering on many grounds of difference. That said, congregations are usually respectful and courteous towards their church leaders, for they remain indisputable authority figures in a particular sphere of existence. But that does not mean that church attendees reveal an ounce of their innermost thoughts to their own clergy. A good-humoured smile; a friendly handshake; and a complimentary exchange of words are meaningless in themselves.

The church as an institution is unquestionably held in some awe and respect, as otherwise it would not have a following. Church-going clearly has a motivation but it may be so vague as to be almost indefinable, beyond its social bonding value, or that religion is vaguely accepted as beneficent. But what does the average church-goer know or believe about the dogmas of the church, and how do these affect him – if at all? In what way - if at all - does church-going improve the character or good behaviour of each individual member of a congregation? These are impossible questions to answer. They are questions that need not be worrying in themselves, but at the present time they are a cause of anxiety for the reason that the leading churches are now in a state of interregnum and uncertainty. That is, they are suspended between the old conventional mindset of the past, and the need to firmly adopt a new thinking for a stable future.

The existence of the churches is as essential today to the majority as they ever were in the past. But they need a new rationale for their existence so that ordinary people might comfortably justify their existence without embarrassment to themselves or to both friends and strangers on reasonable grounds. If the truth be admitted – and the clergy should be the first to accept the fact – the majority of church-goers, together with the majority of non-church-goers who nonetheless choose to label themselves as Christians, do not care a fig for comprehending the doctrines of the church. They may be prepared to give them a nodding assent, but their interest goes no further than that. They may believe or not believe in God, and if the former, they may have no comprehension of his meaning. If they disbelieve in Hell, so may the majority of the clergy, in following theological beliefs already developed in the 19th century; and if they believe in Heaven, they are quite happy to accept their fanciful imagination of that place.

For all the above reasons, it may be said that the majority of Christians, Jews, and adherents of some other religions, throughout Western Europe, and irrespective of whether or not they practice their faith, have already reached the frontier of Deistic belief, or are unknowingly already full-fledged Deists. A modern Deism would define the Deity not as a being but as an immanence, or the evolving of the good as a moral imperative in the ongoing struggle for a better world for humankind and the cosmos. God in this sense is an ethical force for pure goodness, incapable of evil. He may be understood in commonsense terms as a rational being, with no element of revelation, metaphysical gymnastics, or superstition, to explain his existence.

A God interpreted as the original cause of all that occurs in the universe contradicts morality and goodness, for original sin or deserving punishment needs to be invented to explain every evil or accidental misfortune. And in more recent and kinder times deserving punishment has been replaced by theological trickery that amounts to nonsense and convinces nobody. Belief in a Deity who exerts or allows for the existence of evil is unacceptable to modern thought, and the only justification for such a belief in the past was the punishment for inexplicable sin, but the consequence of such a stance cancels out the belief in a loving and discretionary God.

Hence Deism as a philosophy rather than a theology may penetrate all religions in the contemporary world, not as a teaching imposed on the masses, but as a spontaneous and natural process of intellectual thought in meeting the demands of modernity. Most significantly, Deism will not only accept all religions as they are, and transform them discreetly and unobtrusively to serve the interests of a rational God, but contribute towards a universalism in uniting humankind towards a common practical and ethical outlook.[6]

---

[6] For a more comprehensive understanding of Deism, see my book, *Deism and Social Ethics: the role of religion in the third millennium.*

CHAPTER 4
Muslim and Non-Muslim Civilisations

"Religion spurn'd a various rout
Of petulant capricious sects,
The maggots of corrupted texts,
The first run all religion down
And after every swarm its own."

Samuel Butler, *Hudibras*, Pt. III, Canto 2, 1. 8.

The previous chapter summarises the religious situation of our civilisation as we find it at the crossroads today. It has much more to accomplish, and the trials and tribulations that have been overcome successfully since the Reformation still leave little reason for complacency when glancing at the present situation on the world stage. Nonetheless, the European example may hold the key to resolving present problems. We must now return to the question of Islam, make helpful comparisons between the two civilisations, and search for constructive solutions.

In earlier chapters we have made some obvious comparisons between Islam and modern civilisation that point out differences between the two. These are helpful for an introductory perspective of the problem, but they do not begin to explain why Islamic peoples, especially those of the Middle East and the Indian subcontinent, think so differently from those not belonging to their faith. Why do they have an uncompromising attitude to their beliefs and practices; why are terrorist acts blessed by the virtue of martyrdom; and why is it morally imperative that ancient monuments and art works should be destroyed?

The Muslim is able to produce rational explanations for all these practices – or at least, according to the rational understanding of his particular worldview. Rational may not be the best word to use in this context. "Explanation" might be the better term, but "Rational" emphasises the commanding meaning of what *must be* in the light of his ethical thinking. He can conceive of no other alternative. It will therefore be necessary to explore more deeply into the differing thought processes of Islamic and modern civilisations. We have used the term "modern" in contrast to "Western" civilisation in deference to the Confucian cultures of China, Korea, and Japan, to include these countries within the same category.

This is not to deny there are differences between the civilisations of the Far East and that of the West, but the Confucian peoples share certain characteristics that grant them an equality with the West. These are an acceptance of material ethical values in serving the better interests of humanity; a firm belief in reason stemming from those values; a scientific inventiveness, contradicting the old discredited myth that Eastern peoples are only capable of "imitation;" and a love and genius in promoting the arts. Most significantly, the Confucian peoples have never been oppressed by the superstitions of religion, or belief that flattered an enslaved or hopeless condition as occurred, for example, amongst peoples to their West. Buddhism, or other spiritual doctrines emanating from beyond their frontiers, was adapted in coordinating with their own culture.

It was as long ago as the 5th century BC that Confucius circumscribed the desirable limits of religion with the wise remark that "one should respect the spirits but keep them at a distance." This approach towards a Deistic understanding of religion, or the call for secular thought to have preference over the *enthusiasm* of religion, that has wrought such mischief worldwide over the millennia, underlines the practicality and commonsense of Far East civilisation. Most significantly it has emphasised the love of harmony and the need for courtesy in smoothing human relationships.

At the start of the 16th century the technological development of the Confucian peoples was on a par with that of the West. It was the emergence of a decadent pride and the desire for isolation, combined with incuriosity and contempt for the idea that other nations could produce ideas or artefacts of value that threw the Far East into steep decline. First China, and later Japan, closed their doors to the hated "foreigner." But after several thousand years of technological genius and business acumen, it was clear to any intelligent observer that their civilisation had been suspended rather than destroyed. It entered a deathlike sleep. Napoleon was sufficiently percipient to remark, "Beware when the sleeping dragon awakes!" It was not until 150 years after the death of the French Emperor that the sleeping dragon finally awoke to claim his rightful place in the world. And this was not through war or aggression but through dedication to work and a sharp business acumen, and the ability to seize the manufacturing and trading baton of the West.

It would not only be ungenerous but foolish to deny that the Confucian peoples are not on a par with those of Europe or the North American continent or the great Pacific nation states. This is not to suggest that differences in political and social outlook mark a divide between East and West, but the occupational differentiation within a highly technological civilisation forces ahead the need for individualism and ever-higher standards of education, and democratic values follow naturally in their wake.

There was a time when Confucian peoples tended to be relatively dismissive or unconcerned with the humanity of those with whom they had little personal contact. Due to the influences of history over the past 100 years, i.e., social reorganisation, communism, and most recently, the huge increase of major Christian churches in China, there has emerged a more charitable outlook in transforming attitudes. Whilst almost 30% of the South Korean population have statistically been listed as Christian; in Japan it is a mere fraction of that figure, although Christmas has nonetheless become a major festival in that country; whilst in China it has been estimated that as many as 4% of the population may be adherents of the faith – the majority being middle class go-getters who are conscientious believers but maintain a balanced view of reality. It has been estimated that by 2050 China will have the largest Christian population of any country in the world.

The more traditional or quieter forms of Chinese religion need to be noted for purposes of comparison. As in the classical world in the West, their religion is personal in the sense that individuals may choose their own gods to worship according to the inclination that best suits their personality. Entering a Chinese home is reminiscent of entering one of the better houses in ancient Rome, when one is confronted by an altar in the hallway or living room dedicated to the ancestors and chosen gods. Instead of the *penates* (or household gods) the front and sides of the altar are decorated with portraits of ancestors whilst images of the gods are place above. A friend in Malaysia worshipped the Empress Wu, because "she was kind to women," and early every morning she would light joss sticks by the fine porcelain figure of the goddess, and stand a minute or two in silent prayer, before departing for the day to sell Avon cosmetics

The Chinese pray for immediate practical things, as good health and prosperity, tending to have scant regard for remote concerns as "the salvation of souls" or the "forgiveness of sins," and this gives their religion a satisfying utilitarian aspect that is difficult to censure. If it is a religion harking back to ancient thought processes, it nonetheless remains a threat to no one, and does not tend towards the intrusive proselytising tendencies of more modern monotheistic faiths. This is not intended merely as a veiled dig at the threats of Islam, for Christianity, too, has been poisoned by some horrid proclivities. In Britain at the present time there are Christian African churches not only holding a belief in witchcraft but involved in the persecution of those believed to be "possessed by the Devil," and furthermore, have either directly or indirectly, been responsible for the death of small children so accused.

Without wanting to appear overbearing, it may be said that the peoples of Europe, the North American continent, the Confucian and major states of the Southern hemisphere, are enlightened in a particular way that justifies their intercession on behalf of world civilisation to propose guiding principles for a more harmonious future for humankind. It entails a topic of discussion, which whilst it should be equally open for all peoples to participate, calls for a competently placed few to initiate in taking a leadership role. That is, it is a discussion topic that could not be happily resolved by throwing into the arena of a pandemonium of all and sundry, for quarrels of procedure, and semantic misunderstanding, and mischievous elements would break in, in the attempt to destroy the chances for a constructive outcome. In ensuring objectivity and a successful conclusion, such discussion should be led by those experienced and knowledgeable in politics, history, the social sciences, psychology, and religious issues. The following description of the chasm existing between the Islamic and non-Islamic worlds may more clearly explain the reservations expressed above.

No one would choose to doubt the unique place of Islam in the world today although conflicting assessments could be given of its influence and value as a world religion. It originated and developed amongst a culture in a geographical and climatic environment like no other on the planet: on a huge isolated desert peninsula, where day time temperatures in the summer reduce physical exertion to the slowest pace, and in the winter average temperatures equal the hottest days of an English summer. A land with no rivers or lakes, and few oases or wadis, and these at a great distance from one another with limited opportunities for agriculture, presented a land that had always been threatening and dangerous for the travelling groups seeking what passed for pasture for their few goats and camels in sustaining existence.

In this homogeneous environment where one horizon was much like another, and one day followed another in relentless monotony, and the sun rose and fell due to the inevitable power of an unseen agency, there was little to distract the imagination. There were no forests or lakes with their spirits to be propitiated, or the hope for a changing landscape that might transform or improve their earthly existence. Whilst the universe was unchanging (and unchangeable) in its fearful grandeur, as one footstep followed another, there was no knowing what the next day would bring or when the next waterhole would be reached for the relief of thirst. Such harsh conditions naturally engendered an introspection, a tendency towards abstraction, and a positive acceptance of the world as they found it, and this mutated into an awe of wonder at the magnificence of the universe.

Into this world emerged the idea of a single cause: the One and Only God, the Eternal, the Absolute, who begetteth not, nor is begotten. In such a dispersed society of isolated groups, the existence of intermediaries, such as a clergy, was hardly a practical possibility, and so the Deity was viewed as an impersonal God on whom all in their state of human helplessness could call whenever in need or afflicted by distress. The term Allah has no plural or gender, and His nature is beyond comprehension or the possibility to visualise. This was monotheism carried to its furthest limit: that is not a being who had evolved from the national aspirations of a people, as *Yahweh* amongst the Jews; nor as some other tribal leader who through apotheosis is declared a God; nor as the creation of a God through the combining of several concepts, but God as an eternally immutable immanence with no beginning or end.

This principle is important to comprehend, for the Muslim interprets all other religions, despite their pretensions to monotheism, as tending towards polytheism, anthropo-morphism, or some other "infidel" belief. Whilst the Saints of the Catholic Church are deemed as the demi-gods of the Christian Deity, the latter is laughed at as the "three gods in one." The Muslim is never tired of reiterating that, "God has no colleagues." The simplicity and finality of the concept of Allah, and the inexplicable nature of His meaning contributes to the fanaticism driving forward the movement for there is little that allows for open discussion. All is concentrated on command and obedience.

The Koran was revealed to Mohammed by the Archangel, Gabriel, between 610 AD and the Prophet's death in 632 in a somewhat similar fashion to the revelation of the *Book of Mormon* to Joseph Smith 1,100 years later in the United States. Whilst the chronologically earlier Suras or chapters of the Koran revealed at Mecca are primarily concerned with ethical and spiritual matters; the later Medinan Suras concentrate on social and moral issues of relevance to the Muslim community. Of almost equal importance to the Koran is the Hadith recording the sayings of Mohammed, particularly with regard to ideas for the development of Islamic jurisprudence, and it is in this second document that is expressed abhorrence of painting and sculpture of living things, and the stoning of adulteresses.

The most notable characteristic of Islam is that it not only entails a detailed theology, but a system of law, economics, and social behaviour covering almost everyday function of life, such as dress, diet, ablutions, excretory formalities, sexual intercourse, greetings, rules of hospitality, etc. The rules and regulations of Islamic life are not dictated simply to ensure courtesy or order in society but as compulsory religious practices that cannot be evaded or changed under any circumstances. Hence the sermons of religious leaders are often concerned with such matters as the adjusting of the veil, or other pieces of clothing, in differing social circumstances, or the prevention of accidental or bad habits as the exposure of the soles to other persons whilst in a seated position. Such sermons, in both Arabic and English, are readily available for anyone to hear on a selection of Islamic websites.

These compulsory obligations, touching so many aspects of life, not only generate an obsessive psychosis or abnormal fear of wrong-doing, but are so limiting to natural spontaneity that integration is made impossible in meeting the full demands of a free and modern industrial society. Several varied examples in demonstrating the consequences of this may be cited. On one occasion when two students, a Qatari and a Korean were seated at dinner they were treated to the dessert of a chocolate mousse, and the latter who disliked the former read the small print on the plastic cup, exclaiming that the gelatine was derived from pork.

The Qatari, in horror, jumped up from the table and thrusting his fingers into his mouth, vomited into the nearby toilet.

On another occasion when escorting a business partner to his room in a London hotel, we were delayed in the foyer for almost ten minutes as he refused to enter a lift if it was to be shared with "a woman," as in his eyes, he would contravene the law of illegal seclusion – irrespective of the fact that such laws were inapplicable in Britain. On another occasion in Jeddah when discussing social differences amongst a group of business colleagues, one amongst their number remarked on the difficulties of residing in London as the town was full of "naked women" and the mind could not escape the "pollution" of what was presented to the sight. The general view of the Muslim is that the Western world is a place of total promiscuity, and a "Sodom and Gomorrah," since he cannot understand how the view of naked arms and legs (of either sex) cannot but engender a constant lust, seduction, rape and perversions amongst the population. The Muslim imagines the male Westerner to exist in a constant priapic state, whilst the Western woman is everlastingly on heat. It is not sufficient that laws should be instituted against undesirable behaviour; they should also be instituted against undesirable thought.

It is for this reason that so many Pakistanis in Britain in particular have been prosecuted for grooming and abusing underage girls. That is, the latter are already perceived as "fair game" as they reside in a corrupt society already without moral restraint. They are therefore seen as persons deserving little or no respect as effective safeguards in preserving their virginity until marriage is neither guaranteed by their relatives nor others, nor by the established law. The exposure of flesh may be cited as amongst the greatest sins in the Islamic world since it is the cause of most carnal wickedness.

In the light of this in Saudi Arabia Western newspapers are heavily censored, and copies of the *Daily Telegraph*, for example, will arrive at the news stalls with illustrations of naked arms and legs already blacked out. Meanwhile, the *Muttaween* or religious police, armed with their camel sticks, will ensure that those in public areas are not improperly dressed, and men in shorts are liable to be struck across the calves if not placed under arrest. Other indictable offences would be holding hands or kissing between the opposite sexes – although neither of these actions would be deemed offensive if conducted between men only. At the same Jeddah discussion, referred to above, one of the group exclaimed that if any man was to "touch" his sister, he would take up a knife and kill her, and that no one would dare to question the rightness of his action. Such is the definitive judgement of right and wrong. T.E. Lawrence once remarked that the Semitic mind is only capable of distinguishing between black and white, with no room for moderating greys.

CHAPTER 5
Idolatry and differing Spiritual Values

"Four species of idols beset the human mind: idols of the tribe;
idols of the den; idols of the market; and idols of the theatre."

Sir Francis Bacon, *Novum Organum* Summary of the Second
Part, Aphorism 39.

The Islamic attitudes or rules of behaviour, as described above, in themselves have nothing to do with ethics or the reality of a moral society. Only the attitudes and actions of the individual in specific situations can be deemed good or evil. It may be alleged that those categories of non-Islamic peoples as cited in previous pages (i.e. Westerners and Confucian peoples) are morally advantaged and more disciplined than Muslims because of naturally motivated inhibitions and a sense of individual responsibility that frees them from the necessity of multifarious restrictions on their way of life.

These non-Islamic societies are not "dens of iniquity," and although formal institutions as marriage may have lost the significance they once held, the underlying relationships between the sexes, or adults and children, are as safely – or better guarded today than they have ever been. In certain respects, as reflected through the increase in legislation, Western society is more puritanical or strict today than it was in the Victorian era. At that time many examples of gross indecency or sexual abuse, as paedophilia, were not recognised by the legal system – rape alone being almost the only chargeable offence.

The indecency, then rife, often under the guise of hypocrisy, is reflected by reading between the lines of many a Dickensian or other 19th century novel. Today, by contrast, one might cite innumerable situations from earlier epochs that would be quite unacceptable in the 21st century. Hence, when a close analysis is made, it will be seen that the civilised world has advanced rather than regressed in personal morality and behaviour, and this has been achieved through a mass of democratically installed legislation authorised, not by Holy writ but by the will of majorities.

But such comparisons or reasoning would be meaningless to the Muslim who is only capable of following the injunctions of his One God. The Muslim distinguishes between Divine and man made law to a far greater degree than the Western mind has ever adhered to, and with the result that all law must ultimately be traceable to the Divine. And if that is the case, its authority cannot be questioned. And this returns us to the extreme nature of his monotheism or religiosity, for his belief in God excludes a belief in anything else that might detract from the all-consuming power and spirituality of Allah.

This is particularly so with Wahabism and its offshoots, where all ideas or objects must be removed from the possibility of idolatry. Tombs or mausoleums, or burial memorials for the dead do not exist in Saudi Arabia. All are finally laid to rest in anonymous sandy graves – even their kings and notabilities. The same attitude is extended to their history. Their only memory is for the story of their faith as presented in the Koran and Hadith, and for events shortly thereafter, or the quarrels leading to the divisions between Sunni and Shia, or such painful episodes as the Crusades, or memorable triumphs as the fall of Constantinople. All else is held in vanity.

In a certain sense, therefore, the Arabs may be described as a people without a history – or rather, an unbroken chronology of remembered events. It should be noted that India has also been described as "a country without a history," and for similar reasons, i.e., the over-powering force of Hinduism, a very different religion. India, of course, is a country with thousands or tens of thousands of gods, and in no country on our planet can religion be said to have so comfortably accommodated the needs of poverty and its hopeless misery. The wretched put all their energy into religion in rejecting secularism, and so the practicalities and examples of politics and history are often consigned to oblivion. In its place remain the inspiring legends of their gods and the great epics that take on reality for future aspirations. Modern memory, or history seems to stem with the first landings of Europeans at the close of the 15th century. But we must return to the world of Islam.

When I first arrived in Riyadh and met my sponsors on the first occasion, they kindly asked me what I should like to do in the city. I replied I should like to visit the old fortress of the city and see the gate where the great King Abdulaziz had thrust his spear in 1902 at the start of the uprising against the Ottoman Turks. My sponsors momentarily glanced at one another as if I was "mad." This was not what they expected. They had anticipated my wish to see a camel race, or a visit to the gold market, but not the memorial of some "long forgotten" event. I never did get to see the fortress gate and the indentation left by the King's spear. The facts of history were regarded as no more than "time-wasting rubbish" to fill the mind. And the reason for this is that such stories tend towards idolatry.

Idolatry is not simply confined to misrepresenting the notions of God. Correctly defined, it includes the worship of false gods, but it goes on to include anything that excites excessive or supreme adulation. In psychological terms it entails the arousal of spiritual feelings, i.e. of love or inspiration, or reasons for living in greater contentment or happiness. Spiritual feelings may be essential for a belief in God, but their intensity may be as equally strong without any belief in a deity. In the secular world of the contemporary West and the Far East, belief in the arts and our heritage has largely displaced belief in religion as the primary spiritual force uniting us with the cosmos.

In the medieval period, of course, the statues and brightly coloured frescoes of our churches, together with icons and triptychs and elaborate crucifixes over our altars, and stained glass windows and glorious architecture, in themselves inspired deeply aesthetic spiritual feelings as the outward instruments of the organised church. And so they remained until they were swept away by the Reformation as the instruments of idolatry on the grounds of detracting from the true God. But no civilisation has existed without artefacts of beauty in sustaining the spirituality of humankind. When the Orthodox and Catholic churches of the medieval period turned to the beauty of art, they were sufficiently percipient to understand its psychological role.

And so today in the Western world and the Far East, in a religiously sceptical age, we have become increasingly dependent on the arts and literature, and TV costume dramas of the great classics, and historical documentaries, and visits to stately homes, in sustaining our spiritual needs and feelings of being at one with the world. Irrespective of our status or present place in society, we aspire to the values of the heroes and heroines of our classics; and we identity – however distantly – in belonging to the history of those great statesmen, generals, and nobles, who lived in our stately homes. Our souls belong to the nation that made us, and our identity is embedded in the music and culture we love of the civilisation in which we flourish. This may not amount to a true religion but it nonetheless offers a comfort comparable to that of any established church.

All this explains the religious imperative of Isis, the Taliban, Boko Haram, and other Wahabi-inspired movements in consigning to flames the library of the Ahmed Baba Institute, or the destruction of the Bamiyan Buddhas, or the antiquities of Palmyra, since they and their histories detract from the worship of Allah. The millions who visited these places of cultural and historical interest would have viewed their interest as neutral or academic, and would certainly have repudiated the idea that their interest was in any way "religious." But the Wahabi proponents of Isis, etc., may in this context be more psychologically perceptive of the true situation. Everything in existence is either to be worshipped or ignored as too commonplace to attract attention. Expressed another way, everything in existence is either religious or non-religious, and if the former, is either true or false.

The imperative for the destruction of Palmyra and other monuments is not only that they are necessarily idols but that they engender superstition. It is not that the stones are evil in themselves but that the civilisation from which they stemmed was "evil." All civilisations other than the Islamic are held to be irrelevant and a culturally malign influence and hence must be erased from memory. This is the logic of the Islamic mind, and together with other arguments presented above it confirms the totalitarian nature of the faith and its practices and ruthless mode of propagation.

All forms of totalitarianism present an interpretation of causes and lay down rules for every aspect of life. It needs to be clearly distinguished from authoritarianism that may not be ideologically led and may be more arbitrary in its approach. Marxism-Leninism, for example, was clearly totalitarian and amongst the most oppressive of political systems, but it had the one redeeming feature of maintaining a material perspective of the world. Its materialism allowed for the chink of reason to shine through in granting some concrete benefits for humankind, e.g., equality between the sexes, security of employment, and reasonable costs of housing. The totalitarianism of Islam can offer none of these things, nor any equivalent, for its priority of religiosity is at war with almost every aspect of materialism.

Islam demands total obedience to the One God, in both thought and deed, from dawn to dusk, with the promise of a better and more sensuous life in the aftermath of death. This bifurcation between spiritual and material ends is manifested through contrasting modes of psychological discontent. In the non-Islamic world social or individual discontent arises through the oppression of poverty, or dire material need. Uprisings or revolutions occur through economic causes that lend themselves to scientific analysis. In the Islamic world, on the contrary, the causes of discontent take a very different direction due to religious differences. Whilst in the non-Islamic world terrorist acts are almost invariably carried out by anarchist or desperate revolutionaries on the bottom rungs of society; in the Islamic world there appears to be no class differentiation amongst those who resort to violence.

In fact, those responsible for 9/11 and those who founded and promoted the programme of Al-Qaeda, and similar organisations, came from wealthy or otherwise privileged backgrounds. They were in no sense provoked by poverty or material need. Ideology alone was their declared motive, and if deeper psychological motivations are to be sought, they may be found in boredom, alienation and contempt for material existence, and possibly, most of all, in a suppressed sexual frustration and in the impossibility of experiencing the natural functions of a fulfilled life. A society demanding total segregation between the sexes and goes so far as to evoke the criminal law for breaches of such religious injunctions, is likely to be afflicted by many kinds of psychosis.

Westerners are astonished when they read about highly educated doctors and others, who never previously revealed signs of "extremism," and appeared normal in their outward behaviour, then unexpectedly engage in acts of violence or turn themselves into a living bomb. Likewise, there is astonishment when schoolgirls flee from their London homes to join Isis in Syria to fight the cause against the "infidels." The surprise of the parents is still more astonishing, and shocking in a certain sense, when they pitifully plead their daughters were never exposed to an "extremist" home environment. It seems never to have occurred to these elders that the mildest exposure to an Islamic influence is sufficient to tip the balance, and when the propaganda of websites is added to the mix, a greater certainty of decision is given to such commitment.

The psychological dimension must also be noted: sexual tension is bound to accumulate amongst young Islamic women who on one hand are kept in a strict regime within the four walls of their home; and on the other hand are exposed to witnessing the free life of their peers in the outside world. In such a situation these healthy fast-developing teenagers are bound to be attracted by the unmissable romantic opportunity of an early marriage with heroic fighters for the great cause. Meanwhile, there is also a great attraction for those Islamic martyrs. The promise of 56 virgins in the heaven to which they ascend ensures sensuous pleasures on a scale they could never hope to enjoy through a terrestrial existence. The Islamic afterlife is very different from that anticipated by the Christian, and the stark reality of the former in its impression on the imagination goes far in removing the fear of death.

All this creates a situation whereby it is impossible to guarantee that no young Muslim, howsoever mild, self-effacing, or harmless in outward appearance or behaviour, might sometime not engage in a horrific act of violence. In such a cultural milieu none can escape the horrid taint of suspicion, and this poses a huge issue for the non-Islamic world that must somehow be resolved.

Equally remarkable are those instances when men and women from Christian, agnostic, or other non-Islamic backgrounds convert to the faith and then engage in terrorist acts, or otherwise demonstrate a fanaticism that outbids the enthusiasm of Muslims born and bred. The blame is usually placed on the subtle propaganda of Islamic websites, or clever "grooming" by proselytising friends and neighbours, but this is not entirely a satisfactory explanation. It is far more probable that such converts were already alienated from relatives and others in the community, and if not from broken homes, came from those that were already barren in terms of both culture and religion. Through a natural psychological instinct they were in search for spiritual inspiration, and so in their naivety became enmeshed in a spider's web.

Muslims reading the above paragraphs may scoff at all references to "psychology" as a horrid thing at all times in conflict with the principles of religion. Such an attitude need not be exclusive to Islamic people – or at least, not historically. When my generation was at school in the 1940s and early 50s, psychology was the overwhelming influence on our lives and we would give a Freudian interpretation to every act and statement when encountering a clash of opinion. But the home environment was very different where many of our elders (especially amongst the male population) railed against psychology not only as "unproven nonsense" in itself, but as an unwarranted intervention into religious belief and principles.

Such unenlightened views were not only expressed by churchmen and teachers, but even by scientists and those in the medical profession who should have known better. And now, more than 60 years after that period, no same person in the Western or civilised world would question the fact that psychology in necessarily the primary study for understanding humankind to which all other disciplines need to defer. Even economics, as long ago argued by Bertrand Russell, needs to defer to the psychological study of the mind, for only by such a method may one come closest to ascertaining the truth.

It may be that Islamic and non-Islamic societies have an equal measure of self-discipline but the latter is attained in quite different ways. If, however, the question is broached as to which society has the greater tendency towards lawbreaking, or expressed more broadly, the tendency to contravene rules and regulations, a different answer may occur. Because of the huge number of rules and regulations in all advanced industrial economies, and because of their constant amendment and increase, it may be argued that Westerners, etc., are more intentionally self-disciplined out of the necessary circumstances of every day life. Several examples may be cited for such an argument. Firstly, the standard of driving in the Gulf is amongst the most reckless anywhere to be found, and so too are the number of accidents despite the severity of the law. To stand on a zebra crossing is to invite vehicles to increase and not reduce their speed. Cars in Saudi Arabia are fitted with safety belts (because that is the way they arrive from the factory), but if a front seat passenger fastens his belt he will offend the driver. This is because God and not the safety belt would ensure the safety of the passenger during that particular journey.

I experienced a far worse example of disdain for Western-style safety measures in Yemen. Whilst a taxi driver was tanking, one of the six passengers in the vehicle wound down the back window and flicked hot ash onto the petrol pump. This was in San'a where accidental explosions had already destroyed eight filling stations. The response of the government was not to ban smoking in risky areas (deemed an impossible regulation due to the inveterate habit), but to place garages on the periphery of towns away from built-up sites. Again, it should be noted that God is the author of all disasters, and that infringements on the right to smoke should not be seen to interfere with the will of the Deity.

Hence, whilst God-made Sharia law or age-old customs are held in high regard, the man-made rules and regulations of the West tend to be held in mild disdain or even ridicule. None of this should indicate that Muslims or non-Muslims are either better or more moral – or even more law-abiding than the other, but only that there exists a divide in the mode of thinking between the two types of authority.

Before returning to the issue of resolving the problem of Islam, there is another question that calls for an answer. What are the underlying historical causes that have marked the different paths and outcome of Christianity and Islam? And how are these causes significant in addressing the contemporary problem? Although there were other and far more ancient civilisations on the Arabian peninsula, such as Thamud, Sheba, and the Himyarite Kingdom and Awsan, Islam emerged in a relatively simple and primitive desert community by comparison with the great civilisations to their north. The greatest significance of Arabia is that it is the original homeland of the Semitic peoples who emerged in conquering waves and settled the lands of the Near East. The Islamic Arabs were the last of these invading peoples, and they extended their conquests over a far greater territory than any of their predecessors.

Their greatest cultural asset was the development of their language into a powerful literary medium in capturing the imagination of the people and transforming it into a weapon of religious propaganda. It is probable that no one individual in history has exerted a greater power in controlling the personal lives of so many over so long a period of time as the Prophet Mohammed. His control over the habits of daily routine far extended that of Jesus or any other great religious leader of the past. It is unlikely he could have generated sufficient impetus in creating such a religion in imposing his personality on society in the more sophisticated cultures of the time as existed in the

Byzantine or Eastern Roman Empire, or on the complex and warring peoples of the Dark Ages in Western Europe.

The particular homogeneity of the desert peoples surrounding Mecca and Medina, and the confused and unhappy situation amongst the mixed religious influences of paganism, Judaism and Christianity, offered Mohammed a unique opportunity that he seized with alacrity. The central purpose of his life was to comprehend the truth as it could be drawn from the better religious ideas of his time, and then to propagate that truth through the most effective psychological methods in capturing the minds of the majority.

Whilst the power and beauty of the Arabic language raised to its highest literary perfection, and delivered with resounding vocal effect, or in the form of hypnotic chant, was to capture the aesthetic imagination and sensitivity of all; the imposition of repetitive formalities on a daily basis as a moral imperative, was to complete the picture for the organisation and success of a world-conquering faith. It is unlikely that such a religious organisation could have so soon or so effectively been constructed in a more sophisticated or centralised society with all the paraphernalia of bureaucratic mechanisms, but because there was a kind of vacuum or yearning for change at that particular time, Mohammed was free to conceive the most tremendous ambition in capturing the imagination of all to serve the beneficent will of the One God.

It was not until the religion had built up a sufficient head of steam that the *Jihad* of its armies was ready to embark on an invincible adventure of victory that none could challenge effectively. By that time Islam was already a totalitarian organisation, for there was no distinction between church and state, or between religious and secular authority. The fact that all authority was traceable back to the One God defined the nature of its totalitarianism. Whilst the controlling dialectic of East bloc Communism was dialectical-materialism; the dialectic of Islam is (and always was) Divine authority, which in practical terms repudiates the idea of man-made law. This means that Sharia is a fixed system of law remaining for all time, and may never be questioned or changed because it is enshrined in Holy writ – usually in the writings of the Hadith.

The judges or Qadis of Sharia are hardly lawyers in the Western sense, but rather religious functionaries. This means that their grasp of forensic issues is weak, to say the least. For example, in ascertaining the truth of evidence, the word of a Muslim will have priority over that of a non-Muslim, or the word of a man over that of a woman. Hence the search for hard evidence in proving or disproving a case is limited by the religious aura that penetrates the entire system of law. It is rather reminiscent of the primitive law in the Dark Ages or early medieval Europe, when guilt was established through the effects of walking across hot embers, or in throwing a bound person into a lake and witnessing as to whether he would float or sink. The injustice of Sharia law is not so much to be found through its horrific penalties (although those are severe enough) as through its woeful approach to questions of evidence.

It is because the religious mind puts all its trust in the nebulous conception of *faith*, whilst the secular mind demands the use of *reason* with all its demands for concrete proof, that religiously dominated regimes have always been notorious for injustice and cruelty. And whilst all totalitarianism is a moral evil, religious totalitarianism is the most oppressive and cruel of all.

Shortly after the death of Mohammed, quarrels broke out as to the precedence of those who should lead the faith and this led to the split between Sunni and Shia. Loose comparisons have often been made between the Sunni as the "Protestants" of the Islamic faith, on account of their more puritanical approach, and Shia as the "Catholics" because of their memorials and more liberal approach to the decorative arts. Their animosity towards each other is no less intense at the present time than that of Protestants and Catholics in 16th and 17th century Europe. In addition, each are divided into conflicting sects: Sunni being divided into at least 6 major branches; whilst the Shia are divided into 15.

All this helps explains the tenacity of the internecine quarrels between the different groups that are often beyond the understanding of professional peacemakers working for international bodies, let alone the ordinary public who look on in horror. Hence the crisis in Syria and the surrounding territories is not only inexplicable but un-resolvable through efforts at a commonsense approach. As we have earlier observed, the most significant power of Islam at the present day is the influence of Wahabism as manifested through its many offshoots that have mutated into terrorist organisations.

Some observers have described Wahabism as the equivalent of Islam's "Reformation," but this is not an accurate comparison, for although it originated as a revolt against abuses and the laxity of observance of an earlier epoch it progressed along its own ascetic course without dividing into numerous conflicting sects with differing theological ideas. The significance of the Reformation in Europe is that the opening of the Bible for the free interpretation of the common man or woman led eventually to ideas of secular freedom, and by an inescapable process to an age of reason and then to the Enlightenment. Wahabism, on the other hand, has only had the effect of narrowing the intellectual vision of its adherents and then hardening into an unchanging mode of fanaticism intolerant of the outside world.

CHAPTER 6
Russian Religiosity and East/West Values

"Religion converts despair, which destroys, into resignation, which submits."

Countess of Blessington, *Commonplace Book*.

In turning to the West, with its Latin Christianity, we uncover very different foundations for the development of society. The Catholic Church was never absolutist in a political sense, although it may often have claimed an absolutist authority over society. During its earlier period, during the decline of the Roman Empire in the West, it was confronted by invading hordes of Huns, Goths, Visigoth, Vandals, and other barbarians, some of whom were pagans and others adherents of Arianism or other heretical Christian sects.

Hence the power struggles of the Church were external as well as internal. At a later period, during the many centuries of feudalism, the power of the Church was balanced against the militarism of powerful princes and dynasties, and most notably by the drawn out conflict between the Guelphs (supporters of the Papacy) and the Ghibellines (supporters of the Holy Roman Emperor).

Whilst the Church may have dominated learning, in all its branches, throughout the Middle Ages, there were other aspects of society that were strictly secular in attitude. By the 14th century there were no inhibitions against laughing at the foibles of the Church, as reflected, for example, in Chaucer's *Canterbury Tales*, and before that time there had been open rebellion against the Church, on the one hand by quarrelling princes, and on the other through the popular formation of such sects as the Cathars, Lollards, and Hussites. Whilst the pressures of war and dynastic conflict between one territory and another were the major forces driving ahead the demands of invention and science in Western Europe, it was inevitable that secular thought would increasingly displace religious ideas of authority.

With increasing demands on brainpower and the love of knowledge for its own sake, traditional class barriers were gradually undermined, and through an inevitable logic, different forms of freedom were demanded by an ever-widening circle of the community. The achievement of such progress could never have been won through the retention of church authority, as the restrictive prohibitions of the latter would have blocked speculation or imaginative thought at every step on "moral" grounds, i.e., in overstepping the bounds of custom as enshrined in Holy writ.

This principle of secularism versus religiosity for advancing both technological progress and personal freedom is applicable worldwide throughout the ages. Macaulay long ago argued that what he described as the Teutonic peoples were more advanced than those to the south on account of the greater freedom allowed by Protestantism. If Caucasian peoples across the northern hemisphere and their brothers and sisters in the Confucian lands of the Far East, are the most secular peoples on our planet; it may also be argued conversely that the Islamic peoples are the most religious, and that that factor alone is withholding their natural right to technological progress and individual freedom.

In further advancing this argument, we might cite another civilisation that occupies a middle position between Islam on the one hand, and the West on the other. And that civilisation is Russia. Most Europeans instinctively categorise Russia as belonging in a general sense to the European tradition – and would certainly prefer to do so in expressing a closer affinity in the hope of better friendship and closer political links. But Arnold Toynbee, in his massive 12-volume study of the rise and fall of civilisations, has demonstrated clearly that Russia as a civilisation is quite separate from the West, and that this is due to religion or Orthodox Christianity.

Apart from the theological differences of the Great Schism between the churches of East and West in 1054, the main organisational differences between the two is that whilst the Roman Catholic Church retained its own independent authority within the Papacy, the Greek Orthodox Church was integrated within the political system of Byzantium or the Eastern Roman Empire. In early Russia, on the other hand, whilst the church remained all-powerful and ultimately answerable to the Patriarch of Constantinople, it remained independent of the state. Subsequent to the fall of the Empire to the Ottoman Turks in 1453, Moscow was declared as the Third Rome, hence laying its claim as the primary centre of world Christianity. A major shift in power relationships occurred in 1666 when the Patriarch Nikon was deposed by the Tsar Alexis and the church placed under state control.

This move was further strengthened in 1721 when Peter the Great abolished the Patriarchate entirely, so making the church effectively a department of government, ruled by a Most Holy Synod composed of senior bishops and lay bureaucrats appointed by the Tsar. This move was to strengthen every secular act of state authority in undermining the possibility of a future claim by the masses to an extension of individual rights. That is, the God-given prerogative of the ruling powers diminished the petitioning appeal of the ordinary population and seemingly gave an additional moral sanction to tyranny.

There was to be no European Enlightenment east of the river Neisse, and the last gesture for political reform emanating from French Revolutionary ideas was finally crushed with the defeat of the Decembrists in 1825. This had entailed an attempt by the nobility in league with the army to overthrow Nicholas I, the most reactionary of all the Tsars. Shortly thereafter, the organisation of a discussion group was sufficient to incur the death penalty, as experienced by Dostoevsky and his friends who were reprieved at the last moment, after blindfolds had been removed, and their sentences commuted, through the mercy of the Tsar, to 10 years labour in Siberia followed by military service.

The awesome ritual of the Orthodox Church, and the golden beauty of their interiors and the paintings of saints, together with the resounding chanting of priests holding a-high the Gospels or the Crucifix, and the singing of the choir hidden behind the great screen, all contribute to making their religion possibly the most seductively hypnotic and all-embracing of any to be found. Services are conducted almost as a theatrical event, with the congregation standing passively, and only responding with the occasional holy crossing, or deep genuflections that to the Westerner are more reminiscent of worshippers in the Mosque. The great screen has doors to the left and right, through which priests and bishops enter and exit during various stage of the service; and huge double doors in the centre that are fully opened during the climax to reveal the altar to the congregation bathed in the blinding light of a thousand candles.

This is a ceremonial display that far outshines any attempts to impress by the Roman Catholic Church. But the religiosity of the hypnotic ritual should not be allowed to overpower the senses or judgement of the rational being. The Orthodox Church should not be judged by the outward appearance of how it seems, but by what it *is*. That is, it should be assessed within its sociological reality as an institution in society. Its magic is to be found in its annihilating any attempt at a secular interpretation of life, and this leads to the arousing of strong emotions in all decision-making. This in turn leads to extremism and violence that is excused or blessed through the necessity of *right*, and this is irrespective of whether we refer to the Holy Russia of the Tsars, or the Atheist Russia of Soviet Communism.

Although Tolstoy and Dostoevsky are often recognised as the foremost novelists of the world, and none can question their genius in the psychological penetration of character, their dramatic power, and their vivid and moving picture of life covering all levels of society, on the other hand, both men loathed and despised the West and all its values. Whilst Dostoevsky retained a steady opinion through most his creative life, Tolstoy became increasingly critical and unrealistic in his view for a better world with the advance of old age. The critique of both men and of many other thinkers in Russia and beyond, and irrespective of religiosity or none, is that they believed in the moral perfectibility of humankind, and they failed to comprehend that the belief in such a principle when transformed to the political sphere would lead inevitably to the worst kind of tyranny and totalitarianism of one kind or another.

This is because the drive to moral perfection evokes intolerance and the need for unquestionable authority. Humankind, or individuals, are neither good nor bad, but a mix of both, and in recognising the reality of this in a free society, it should not be the function of the state to force the individual into a straitjacket of its own moral mould, but rather to direct undesirable or unsocial characteristics, as aggression, greed, or uncooperativenesss, etc., into occupational spheres that benefit the broader community. This is the contrast between the alternative tyrannical and democratic modes in best utilising the energies and inclinations comprising the widely diverse characteristics found within any population.

West Europeans, and indeed most informed people worldwide, respect the Russian culture with its music, literature, and other arts, and are in awe of their great artists and performers. The underlying technique of their music and literature is clearly European, even though the inspiration arises from their national spirit and particular mindset. But most Europeans have little understanding of the Russian mentality, or have only been exposed to the superficiality of jovial gatherings or friendly drinking sessions, or the formality of business negotiations, when pleasant enough encounters are experienced.

But real differences remain. It was not enough for Peter the Great (denounced by the Old Believers as the Antichrist) to bring French and Italian architects and sculptors to build his Window on the West, or for Catherine II to invite a few *philosophes*, as Diderot and D'Alambert, to grace her Court in St. Petersburg, in magically transforming Russia into a Western state. When a non-Russian reads a Dostoevsky novel for the first time, he is struck by the oddness of the characters and may exclaim to himself, "But this is unreal – people don't behave like that!" But they do. The sudden mood swings, the unpredictability, and the violence of the Russian temperament followed by humiliating self-abasement, contradicts the principles of self-control which directs the Westerner towards a more restrained mode of behaviour. One moment the Russian is engaged in an outrage he immediately regrets, and the next he is kneeling in tears, praying before an icon.

The instinctive response of the Westerner to such tendencies, and irrespective of whether it is in fact or fiction is disdain at such prostration. There are situations when forgiveness or exculpation from blame cannot be easily granted to those who overstep the mark – or so thinks the Westerner in his more mundane and cooler approach to life. The Westerner who commits sins or crimes is more concerned with the immediate practical outcome of earthly punishment than the prospect of God's displeasure.

When in Russia in 1962, at the height of the Cold War, I witnessed the reality of several such perverse incidents. Shortly before a marriage ceremony I saw a drunken father verbally abuse his son, the groom, as several guests tried to intervene and others quarrelled amongst themselves in acting out a disgraceful scene. On another and very different occasion, on emerging from a packed cathedral after an Easter service, I encountered thousands of genuflecting worshippers kneeling in the melting snow as hundreds of beggars and cripples plied for alms, and others sold candles and amulets – and this was a country in which the authorities alleged that "beggars and cripples did not exist."

Although Stalin allowed the re-opening of the churches in 1941 to play their part in the Great Patriotic War, Khrushchev closed 12,000 of them in the late 1950s. For centuries the country was referred to as Holy Russia. All the efforts of the Communist regime over a period of 70 years to impose atheism through persecution, ridicule, and every effort to discredit religion was all for nought if the post-1989 resurgence of religiosity is taken into account. And in return, it may be asked, what view does the Russian have of the typical Westerner?

The Westerner is seen as a "cool fish," who either has few feelings or suppresses them, who is ungodly, and worships the counting house with its ledger for entering profits and loss. In other words, the commonsense values of prudence in accumulating capital for a better standard of living or for a "rainy day," are held in disdain in reflecting a trifling or humdrum personality in lacking the kind of ideological fervour that so inspires the Russian mind. But what use is ideological fervour if it means little more than abstruse religiosity, or what is equally reprehensible, if it is turned into an abstruse secular ideology of questionable practical value? Holy Russia or Communist Russia, they are both alike with their differing superstitions. More admirable are the down-to-earth ideals of the practical prudent life with a sound sense of self-interest and self-preservation, as depicted, for example, in that greatest of thought-provoking books, Daniel Defoe's *Robinson Crusoe*. Published in 1719, this adventure story still portrays the type of wisdom that every sensible and free Westerner should aspire to. The most free and best organised societies are best attained through laying emphasis on cultivating the virtues of the individual rather than those of the collective that may so easily be used by the state for oppression.

Perhaps, in retrospect, it is unjust to blame the Russian for the faults or failings of his character. It may be that historical circumstances are to blame for his unpredictability or violence in a society that became intolerable for human existence. In a society where there are (or were) arbitrary arrests, and where men may be held without charge, or are ignorant of their offence, or where years of incarceration are endured through disease and privation in appalling conditions, there is bound to be fear, anger, and violence that turns to psychosis. If that is not true, then what kind of suffering turns men to madness?

The Russians are no less sensitive than other peoples and have expressed this in the genius of their art. If the Russian is entirely void of political genius, then again, perhaps the fault should not be turned into a question of blame. His every attempt at free thought or expression has been crushed before his speech was completed, or the ink was dry on the printed page. Those from the middling to the higher echelons of society have often sought to serve the better interests of their people in a spirit of philanthropy, but all to little avail, whilst the masses have remained sunk in a morass or misery.

Further indications of the divide between the Russian and Western civilisations is made evident by the pervasive inferiority complex of the Russian, or his need to overcompensate for what he imagines are slights made on his country or its past. This sensitivity is mixed with a fair degree of suspicion, and a defensive stance adopted whenever a positive reference is made to one's own country that in turn is taken as a veiled attempt at diminishing his own. If a casual reference is made to an object or idea in one's home country, the response is often that he has a bigger or better equivalent.

It is interesting to compare this common attitude with that of another people with a similar recent background of Communist ideology. The Chinese, by contrast, are always self-assured, and so confident of the superiority of their civilisation that they are hardly moved by any suggestion of criticism. Their urbanity, and the good humour of their courtesy, ensures they would neither embarrass themselves nor others by raising a matter of abrasive controversy or responding to such, and in this way a pleasant and equal exchange is maintained. Whilst this may reflect the manners of a relatively new with those of an ancient civilisation, the main point is that the comparison is made between two Communist states at one time supposedly sharing the same ideology and values.

In regard to Russia, it may also reflect a country that for 300 years has aspired to be a truly Western power, but has failed for reasons it cannot quite comprehend. It has perceived the West as somehow a superior civilisation, on account of its technological and material success, and yet it has never been prepared to accept those essential values that underpin such success. Hence it experiences an internal conflict as to how it should adjust its relationship with the West. In view of the long tradition of the Chinese civilisation, by contrast, any such pretensions to Westernisation would simply appear as absurd. The Chinese may aspire to modernisation in terms of creative ideas and technology, but that should be differentiated from a "Western" influence.

In considering the contrast between the Russian and Western mindsets one cannot illustrate the situation with better clarity than by comparing the two civilisations when found existing together cheek by cheek. And here we must turn to the Baltic States and Finland. In the latter I was resident for 9 years in the 1960s, and in regard to the former, I was a visitor to Estonia in 2015. The Finns and ethnic peoples of the Baltic states are amongst the most Westernised of peoples (despite their geographical location) if the criteria of democratic values and institutions in conjunction with the highest educational values sought in developing advanced economies; and freedom within an egalitarian framework, are applied.

It is not surprising that Finland is amongst the most Westernised of countries, as for 600 years she was under Swedish rule, and in the words of the Swedish academic, Carl Hallendorf, since the 18th century, "At a time when political despotism prevailed in Continental Europe, Sweden and England were the only countries where the government acted in cooperation with the representatives of the people."[7]

It may be surprising, however, that the Estonians, Latvians, and Lithuanians should also be included as amongst the most Westernised of nations, firstly, because they never attained independence as nation states until after the First World War, and secondly, because their ethnic populations were under the rule of super-states, predominantly Russia, for the greater part of their recent history. The explanation for this is to be sought in the fact that in the early medieval period the Baltic coastal regions came under the Westernised influence of the Danes, later the Teutonic Order, and then the Hanse League that introduced the legal system of Lübeck to the peoples of the territory. With the Reformation, whilst the Lithuanians remained Catholic, the Latvians and Estonians embraced the Lutheran faith.

---

[7] *History of Sweden*, C.E. Fritze Ltd., 1938, p. 340.

As a result of Sweden's wars with the competing powers of Poland and Russia, the Baltic region became part of the Swedish empire. Benevolent government was installed and an efficient educational system, and at a later age, the Estonians always looked back with longing at what they described as the "good old Swedish days." Whilst the landowners in the Baltic were predominantly German, with a more sparsely spread Swedish aristocracy, the ethnic population worked the land or engaged in fishing or craftsmanship in the towns. With the defeat of Sweden at the battle of Poltava by the Russians in June 1709, the Baltic fell under the rule of the latter where it remained until the defeat of Russia by Germany in the First World War.

Three factors may be attributed to the Western mindset of the ethnic Balts: the long term influence of Germanic legal systems; the cultural influence of the Lutheran Church; and most significantly, the benign and powerful influence of Swedish administration. The three Baltic States enjoyed only 20 years of independence and democratic freedom during which they successfully developed the foundations for modern industrial economies. And then in 1939, with the outbreak of the Second World War, they experienced 50 years of horror under the unmitigated tyranny of Soviet rule. A large percentage of the populations of the Baltic States were arbitrarily taken into custody and transported in cattle trucks to Siberia, where most died of disease, starvation, or were worked to death; and in exchange, large numbers of Russians were transported to fill up the half empty villages and towns. In addition to the usual totalitarianism of ideologically driven regimes, the cultural aspirations of the Balts were cruelly suppressed.

Having briefly described the background of the Baltic situation I now want to relate my personal observations on visiting Estonia, and how it impinges on the peoples of two widely contrasting civilisations existing side by side. At the present time Russians represent 25% of the population, but voluntary segregation separates the two ethnic groups. On a first impression one is surprised by the good humour, friendliness, and optimism of a people on whom so much suffering has been inflicted. One cannot but admire the high quality of their cuisine, their inventiveness in industry, and perhaps especially their innovativeness in designing new modes of banking to serve the peoples of Europe in facilitating cheaper international transfers of currency.

Their view of their Russian neighbours is interesting. Whilst they pride themselves as being the most "non-religious" country in the world (a fact which I questioned on the grounds that churchgoing figures were probably comparable to those of Britain and other West European countries) they were critical of Russians as over-religious and dogmatic. Their resentment of Orthodoxy was probably in part due to the building in 1905 of the huge Alexander Nevsky Cathedral on the Toomba hill dominating the capital Tallinn, as a political statement of Russification – an insulting gesture in a Lutheran country. Whilst Estonians have a modern and liberal attitude to family relationships, they allege that Russians are "old fashioned," authoritarian, and misogynistic, and when wife-beating cases are heard in the courts it was usually Russians who were the defendants. Whilst Estonians were usually good-natured and polite, Russians tended to be "dour and aggressive in every day encounters, and they were not people with whom it was easy to develop a social relationship or conduct an intelligent conversation."

It is rare to meet an Estonian who has not had either a close of distant relative who was not shipped off to Siberia, and who either perished there or returned decades later as a "broken" personality. In Estonia there are many humorous stories about the absurdities of Soviet administration, such as when a stadium was built in Tallinn for viewing the sailing events of the Olympic games, the seating was so arranged that two banks of benches were so constructed as to face one another but out of view of the sea where the competition was held.

It may be noted that the Estonians hold the Finns to the north in high regard, not merely because both speak closely related languages, but because of their role in the Second World

War. Whilst the Baltic states were an "easy walkover" for aggression by the Soviets in 1939, the Finns put up a strong resistance to the invaders, and although they lost 10% of their territory and their second largest city, Viipuri, they nonetheless, as victors in the Winter War of 1939-40, with a population of only 4 ½ million, inflicted a crushing defeat on Goliath.

When the Germans arrived in Estonia in 1941, they were hailed as liberators, and in the words of our Estonian guide, although few of their people had any sympathy for the ideology of the new invaders, as Westerners, they were "people with whom you could relate on an equal and rational basis." The Finns, meanwhile, under the leadership of the Anglophile, Marshal Mannerheim, played an astute part in the War in sustaining their survival: first, through a military alliance with Germany in an attempt to regain their lost territory, and second, in changing sides to support the allies in 1944.

At the peace settlement Finland was forced to pay a huge compensation in kind to the Soviets, but wisely has retained friendly relationships with her eastern neighbour to the present day, whilst also maintaining the largest army in Europe in proportion to her population. Whilst the Finns remain a neutral power (in so far as they can as a EU member), the Baltic States are not only keenly allied to the EU, but are also NATO members. Their vulnerability cannot but give rise to anxiety, and on leaving Estonia it was reassuring to see two US bombers parked in readiness at Tallinn's airport.

CHAPTER 7
American Fundamentalism and Islam's Penetration of the West

"In religion, as in friendship, they who profess the most are the least sincere."

Richard Sheridan, *The Duenna*, Act III, Sc. 3.

The above consideration of the relationship between Russian civilisation and that of the Westernised Baltic States and Finland should not be regarded as a digression from the main topic of Islam's totalitarian threat to world civilisation. Muslims comprise part of the total of humankind, and it is not suggested that those outside their faith are not also exposed to the possibility of inflicting the same or similar ills. This analysis should already have clearly revealed that it is not Muslims as individuals who are inherently in the wrong, but rather the outcome of the *actual* teaching of their religious leaders, and the organisation and culture of the faith.

It is the malign psychological effects of religiosity carried to the extreme that is the subject of this book, and not of religiosity in itself. Religion, in this sense, may be compared to medicine, which is only beneficent if taken in the correct dosage. If it is too little, it is ineffective, and if it is too much, it becomes a poison. It is a question of always maintaining the Golden mean. Of course medicine as with religion may affect the individual in different ways: not only in terms of strength of dosage, but also with regard to side effects. And the latter is particularly relevant in the matter of religion when exposure to excess of religiosity may either create a saint or a suicide bomber.

We have already amply demonstrated the evils to which religion in excess has exerted its power within the Western world in centuries past. We have also shown how the malign influences of religion, or more correctly, the power of religiosity may be transferred into purely secular organisations, for example, when the all-embracing enthusiasm of Russian

Orthodoxy reappears in the tyrannical demands of Soviet Communism. It is the totalitarianism of both that marks them as the bane of society. And at the present time the social and political tensions in Eastern Europe are the heritage of these historical circumstances.

It is sad that for political reasons Russians are feared, despised and loathed, not only in the Baltic States but in all those territories once behind the Iron curtain. It may be true that certain endemic characteristics of the Russian as reticence, an abrasive manner towards strangers, or a cheerless attitude in company, are often attributed to political leanings rather than their natural temperament, and these misconstrued appearances tend to worsen relationships with other nationalities. Hence those impressions of various Estonians, as described in the previous chapter, may reflect an element of misunderstanding. All this goes far in illustrating the harmful rippling effects of irresponsible religiosity.

The moderate or Deistic approach towards religion now found throughout Western Europe, in Catholic and Protestant countries alike, as well as amongst the Confucian peoples of the Far East, is a compliment to both the true value of religion and the sanity of the world. In America, unfortunately, the same situation does not entirely prevail. There is a certain irony in the fact that whilst in Europe religion has traditionally been state-sponsored – and still often is, in America it has been constitutionally excluded from a role within the state, and yet it is in that country where religious enthusiasm is rife and Christian fundamentalism exists.

This is not to deny that the latter exists in Europe also, but only in isolated pockets amongst ill-informed people who are disdained by the majority as eccentric if not a dangerous nuisance. In America, on the contrary, the churches are necessarily highly organised as financially self-subsistent institutions, and it follows that congregations need to be driven in a herd-like fashion on a Sunday regular basis to their places of worship, in generating sufficient income to pay the costs of their messianic preachers and the maintenance of their huge arena-like structures. It would be hyperbolical to suggest that Christian fundamentalism anywhere approaches the degree of threat of its Islamic counterpart, but it nonetheless presents a considerable danger to society and democratic values.

It has already been responsible for the shedding of blood in the war against abortion clinics, and in the political field it has exerted an unpredictable influence in promoting wild or extremist policies. At the same time, the readiness with which American politicians are prepared to call upon the deity is distasteful to Europeans, and quite unacceptable in the more secular ambience of European politics.

The reason for the excess religiosity of the American temperament is usually given to the long tradition of the Puritan fathers who settled New England early in the 17th century. It was the descendants of these people who gave rise to the wickedness of the Salem witch hunting at the end of the same century, at a time in Europe when belief in witches was already long discredited amongst educated people. The political witch hunts of the much later McCarthyite era may also be traced to the same religio-psychological-inspired tradition.

But I believe the Puritan tradition cannot wholly be held accountable for the religiosity we witness in contemporary America. This is because it originated and flourished in a relatively limited location, and many other religious sects exerted an influence in the following centuries as the continent was populated with ever-greater numbers of the impoverished and persecuted from the Old world. I believe the more significant cause for the intense religiosity of contemporary Americans is traceable to a cultural alienation, and inner loneliness of spirit, as so clearly delineated, for example, in the short stories of O. Henry. The environment lacked the strong bonds of history in proudly connecting them with the past, and the uplifting spiritual dimension of an inescapable patriotism.

These are the comforting qualities that have substituted conventional religion in the Europe of modern times. The American, on the other hand, was obliged to invent myths for a new kind of patriotism with its unique rituals, often evoking a smirk from the cynical European. But such myths were not sufficient, or too superficial, to satisfy the spiritual needs of the American, and so resort to an older form of religiosity was needed to fill the gap.

The peoples of Europe, as also of the Far East, draw tremendous strength and a sense of worth from the traditions and thinking of their ancient cultures, and this is lacking in the heterogeneous milieu of such a recent past as in the US. The American tends only to find excitement and inspiration in the immediate present, disdaining the past as insignificant or mildly absurd. Such an attitude is most strongly reflected in the many literary works of Mark Twain. In the political sphere, especially in the post-War period, the unique perception of his own national identity has made him blind to the specific needs of other cultures for recognition and respect. No country is quite like another and all peoples need to hold others in equal regard in valuing their national integrity.

All this should be taken as a reminder that the civilised world cannot remain entirely complacent or self-righteous in its hidden duty to criticise and attempt the amendment of Islamic extremism.

Before attempting to address the problem for the resolution of Islamic fundamentalism, it would first be advantageous, in underlining the urgency of the issue, to look more broadly at the threat to world civilisation. This threat is manifested in many forms and through differing attitudes of thought.

Throughout the world, amongst people of goodwill, the Arab Spring of 2011 was welcomed as a great hope for the future, but from the beginning it was based on ignorance and false optimism and could never have materialised. For a start, the idea of democracy is contrary to the moral precepts of the Muslim and the authoritarian rules guiding every aspect of his life. He may believe in egalitarianism, but that is quite another principle, and if democracy is raised as a theoretical possibility, he may ask, is it politically desirable and how might it be attained? To the modern mind change in society is only achievable through democratic mechanisms, but if these are repudiated as unacceptable, and freedom is denied, then the only alternative is the splintering into power groups, each with the absolutism of its leader, followed by the bloodshed of a chaotic situation. And that has typified the history of Islamic peoples in the contemporary world.

Whilst in the older type regimes of the hereditary Emirates or Kingdoms of the Gulf there may be oppression and little opportunity for free expression, at least there is the consolation of order, relative stability, and safety in the streets. But in the more modern regimes of supposedly elected presidents, as in Iraq, Iran, Syria, Libya, Yemen, or Afghanistan, there is everywhere unpredictability, death and chaos. Although oppression is undesirable and offers little hope for a better future, there is nothing worse than a state of anarchy – even though it may have been inspired through the good intentions of democracy. This illustrates the ignorance of the West of those foreign cultures, and the wrong-headedness of imposing a system that may be suitable in advanced industrial economies but is quite unworkable amongst pre-medieval peoples. This, then, is the extent of the problem to be faced.

The population explosion in the Middle East and North Africa is possibly the greatest underlying threat, not necessarily through the pressures of population in itself, but rather through the changing and distorted pattern in the emergence of dominant age groups. In taking 16 Islamic countries in the Middle East and North Africa, 57% of their populations are under 30 years of age, with Yemen at the top with 74% and the UAE at the bottom with 44%. In taking 12 Islamic countries in the same areas, 24% of their populations are between 15-29 years of ago, with Algeria at the top with 37% and Qatar at the bottom with 13%.[8]

When all the testosterone is calculated for a young male population of hopeless unemployed, deprived by religion from the enjoyment of female company, a ticking time bomb has been set. Where are their energies to be directed? In societies deprived of most the cultural and leisure activities known in the

[8] Figures taken from the *Time* magazine for 28th February 2011.

West as clubs, bars, theatres, cinemas, etc., the only outlet is religion and social gatherings around the mosque. In this way all latent discontent and aggression is directed by the Imams and Mullahs onto the hatred of the "infidel" who is blamed for all the evils of the world.

If the Westerner imagines that the Islamic preacher is comparable to the kindly pastor calmly delivering his Sunday sermon in good humour from the pulpit, he is very far from the mark! Walk past any mosque on a Friday in the Middle East, and listen to the tannoys from the minarets, and you will hear ranting amounting to hysteria. If the words are incomprehensible and the meaning indecipherable, the tone and attitude are sufficiently clear to arouse a shudder of horror down the spine. This is reminiscent of another place in another age. What future goodness could be expected from the younger generation when confronted by the malice of such a religion? The potential for violence is ever-present without the need for a God-driven stimulant.

Although the underlying cause of conflict in the Middle East may be a soaring birth rate, the immediate cause of mass migration from that territory is political anarchy, the destruction of war, and the daily fear of death. The acceleration of migration into Europe of thousands, and then tens of thousands, with the possibility of millions in the near future, has taken governments by storm. This was a crisis that seemingly came from nowhere, at first evoking sympathy, then an open-armed charity, followed by alarm, confusion, and then resistance against the hordes pushing across the frontiers. Migration on such a scale had never been experienced since the *Völkerwanderungen* of two thousand or more years ago.

The emigration of the religiously persecuted of old from one European country to another had long been known for centuries, and the governments of many countries had welcomed the newcomers, but this was different. In earlier times it had almost invariably entailed a cross-cultural exchange, but now it involved a very different civilisation settling in another – and the two were incompatible on several levels. Successful immigration entails the necessity for integration into a new society. That does not entail that old values, beliefs, and customs should be repudiated, but it does entail that outward appearances and manners should be adapted as a courtesy in deferring to the host peoples, and more significantly, in inviting acceptance, ease of contact, and friendship in a strange land.

, European peoples have always reciprocated in welcoming these migrants from a very alien civilisation. They have formulated the theory and tried to put into practice the principles for a *multi-cultural society*, by which is meant a society facilitating ease of movement and cooperation for residents from any part of the planet with the minimum risk of friction. Towards this end, laws against racial discrimination have been enacted; new vocabularies have been invented in formulating *political correctness* in further safeguarding the interests of minorities; official notices have been translated by central governments and local authorities into several hundred languages; housing has been made readily available; financial handouts have been issued in helping the unemployed and indigent; and the right to build mosques on prime urban sites has always been granted.

These gestures of assurance and friendship by nation states and democratic peoples, however, have not been returned by a gesture of gratitude. Why is this? Firstly, the Muslim does not recognise the idea of the nation station, or more correctly, it does not feature in his consciousness as a factor of significance. Of course, in his homeland he may have supported national movements against what he perceived as foreign oppression, but he has never developed a national consciousness, or "love for the soil," or for a distinctive culture, in the European sense. Secondly, the Muslim only seriously recognises his own faith as an over-arching authority embracing all people irrespective of frontiers. These attitudes are manifested in practical ways that alarm Westerners, the cognisance of which Muslims are innocently unaware due to an excusable blindness to the existence of such cultural factors.

The establishment of an Islamic parliament, or moves to create a state within the state, are practical ways in which the Muslim may attempt to exert his political influence. The Westerner is shocked at such an outrage, but prefers to remain silent in the knowledge that such a parliament has no legal jurisdiction and hence is little more than play-acting. When moves are then made to create "No-go areas" in some of our major cities, this arouses a mixture of feelings from anger to confusion, to sympathy – and sometimes to a burst of laughter. The motive for "No-go areas" is to clean up streets of vice or prostitution by harassing girls in skimpy dresses, or ensuring that their own womenfolk are fully veiled for their own "protection." Such interference with people in a public place may wield no legal authority, but again, the officers of the law may wisely turn a blind eye on such episodes for fear of stirring up a hornet's nest.

When Muslims then establish their centres for Sharia law and hold their courts for deciding on personal financial or family matters, or questions of divorces, etc., a step too far has already been taken. It is then that journalists take an interest in what is actually involved, and the police embark on their first enquiries. But the law is a slippery animal to play with, and with its complications and slow procedures, the *Qadis* learned in their own esoteric knowledge, have time to make a fuss and raise a dust storm in their favour.

In 2011, for example, the debate had reached so far that the then Archbishop of Canterbury, Dr. Rowan Williams, even pleaded for the acceptance of Islamic law in certain sectors of its reach. It may be decades before adulteresses are stoned to death in Bolton or Bury, or homosexuals are beheaded in Huddersfield or Halifax, but there are *Qadis* and Mullahs now living and working in Britain, who are hoping for that day and are agitating patiently towards its eventual realisation.

Not contented alone with the above interventions into the established modes of English life and law in gaining privileges specific to themselves, Muslims have at the same time maintained a quite unreasonable outcry against alleged "discrimination" and "persecution" at every turn in their progress, and at every opportunity. Every compliance with their wishes has emboldened their confidence with ever more complaints against those who feed their wishes. These have veered from cries of humiliating self-pity to roars of anger against those raising the first gesture of opposition. None of the above attitudes or behaviour would even occur to Muslims if it was not for the fact that "Islam alone in the world is worthy of respect and authority." If that was not their view of existence their self-righteousness would be seen in *their* eyes as either arrogance or impudence.

In view of the above allegations it would be apt to transpose the above situation, and suggest how things might be if the Westerner were to make similar demands in the spiritual heartland of the Muslim's homeland, Saudi Arabia. It should be noted that the Westerner has no rights in that country, which no person may enter without the invitation of a sponsor and the issuing of a visa. Non-Islamic religious practices publicly displayed are subject to punishment. The carrying of a prayer book in the hand may result in a public flogging. No Caucasian may yet have suffered this penalty but a Filipino has.

The visitor to the country is anxious over the dereliction of its customs, fear of the *Muttaween* or religious police, and never quite certain whether his Exit visa will be issued on time without which he cannot leave the country. One occasionally encounters the Westerner, around the hotel pool during the siesta period, who experiences the nightmare of being trapped for days in the country because of clearance difficulties for his departure. A query over a letter of credit or delays over a shipment may lead to the stress of a Kafka-like situation.

Whilst Caucasians feel relatively secure, other races are very vulnerable and subject to appalling treatment – particularly foreign women in domestic service – and Islam is a religion supposedly free of racial discrimination. Stories have circulated of Thai or Filipina women who have lost hands or arms through convictions arising from the allegedly false accusations of their employers.

This demonstrates clearly, if it was ever necessary to make the point, that whilst the Muslim in Europe or elsewhere is granted the right to enjoy every freedom abroad, no such equal rights are reciprocally granted to non-Muslims in Islamic states. In a world where equal rights are respected, if Muslims are permitted to build mosques in Bradford of Barnsley, then why should not Christians be permitted to build churches in Mecca or Medina? Is not the soil of the Englishman, or that of any other nationality, as sacred to him as the soil of Arabia is to any Muslim?

The difference, of course, is that the Muslim, through the over-whelming authority of his One God, insists on an absolute right over the feelings or claims of any other group on our planet. All must pay obeisance to his irrevocable demands. The problem arises, of course, when the world recognises these demands and claims for rights, and is prepared to fulfil them in so far as is possible. And all the world is thereby confronted with an awkward or embarrassing situation in maintaining tact and diplomatic good manners.

It is then that the nation state, through which majorities or ordinary people live out the experience of their political life are placed under impossible pressures. This is particularly so in democracies where people enjoy equality of rights. When such societies are penetrated by a foreign group that not only refuses to integrate but is uncompromising in pursuing customs and modes of behaviour incompatible with the host country and furthermore, are determined either covertly or overtly, to overthrow the culture of that country, what resources of defence are allowed in combating this attrition?

CHAPTER 8
How Islam Exploited the West's Crisis of Confidence

> "A man's 'religion' consists not of the many things he is in doubt of and tries to believe, but of the few he is assured of, and has no need of effort for believing."
>
> Thomas Calyle, *Latter-Day Pamphlets*, No. 8.

As illustrated below, a number of vital philosophical principles are raised in resolving the incompatible divide as to how Muslims and non-Muslims might live together without conflict in the same society. In a peaceful modern industrial democracy the politicising or discussion of religious issues should never need to occur. Religion should be a private matter only of concern to the individual, and that is how it has been in the West and throughout the Far East over the past two hundred years.

But today religion has become the hot topic that it should never be. And this has certainly not occurred due to any desire on the part of Westerners, but rather due to inevitable and accidental forces arising from a clash of rights and obligations in a democratic environment. In shorthand, it has occurred when the lid is pressed down on the boiling pot of *political correctness*, or when the latter bites back at the philanthropists who have attempted to legislate for a more just or fairer society.

Old and long-forgotten quarrels are regurgitated, or dug up and given a new lease of life as a defensive measure in responding to new threats. Religion once again takes on an ugly pose, and in being politicised marks the regression rather than the progress of society. Politically inspired religious disputes are not only time wasting in themselves but harmful to a sound political environment. They are not only anachronistic but poisonous to good social relationships. But circumstances have arisen whereby the politicising of religious issues is forced upon the non-Islamic peoples of the world against their will.

As a result of this, established democratic principles are not only called into question but are forced into reversal, but not to the detriment of democracy but for its defence. If this sounds paradoxical the explanation is to be found in the fact that a War situation has been created. Such a war need not be defined in the conventional terms of armies marching against one another, but rather in the sense as declared by the French President, François Hollande, after the Paris massacre. It is defined in the sense of a clash between un-compromisable groups, when one enacts (if not actually declares) its enmity against another with the eventual intention of reducing it to submission. The war takes the form of ongoing attrition through propaganda in mosques, on websites, and through lobbying for ever-more privileges, or the subtle introduction of sharia-like regulations into the established legal systems of nation states.

The leading democratic principles that are called into question are: 1) That all in society should be treated as equals; 2) Positive discrimination in assisting weaker, minority, or less privileged groups a more equal opportunity with those more fortunately place; and, 3) Discriminatory laws of any kind intended against a specific group or type of abuse, which then inadvertently oppresses long-established cultural associations or their worthwhile values. None of these principles should be regarded as absolute but rather as relative and applicable to particular situations within the constitutional framework of the nation state. Examples will be cited below, and it will be demonstrated how the first steps have inadvertently, or even unknowingly, already been taken to undermine or destroy the modern civilisation of the world.

The following specific areas of activity will be taken in turn: 1) Islam's cultural threat to the West; 2) Islam and the curbing of free speech throughout our universities; 3) The threats against Christianity; and, 4) The failure of the police to act against Islamic threats.

1) Islam's Cultural threat to the West

Islam would not be a cultural threat to the West, or in a wider sense, to world civilisation if it was not for the fact that the former has lost confidence in itself and in its proper and desirable purpose in the world. This loss of confidence in its value and will to power, as a force for good, stems from a number of causes. Firstly, a false consciousness of guilt has arisen in regard to our imperial past. I describe this as a false consciousness as it would be absurd to argue that our colonial past was motivated by malice. It was motivated by the desire for profitable trade in benefiting both sides in a bargain, and in circumstances that were unprecedented and could not be anticipated.

Unknowingly to the broader population of the dominant parties, it led to mistakes, faults of judgement, and occasionally to inexorable criminality. These facts have long been recognised and the guilty parties damned by history, but once that recognition has been openly assented to, there is no reason for living generations to harbour feelings of guilt. On balance, we should celebrate the benefits of our imperial past for all the material and cultural benefits and opportunities, scientific and other, we have brought to humankind on a global scale.

The above situation of guilt has in turn led to a compensatory deference to overseas peoples whereby they should hurriedly be granted any or all demands and rights, irrespective of prudential considerations or the anticipated consequences of such demands. In other words, rights were granted in exchange for shedding any further responsibility for the future of such peoples, and in this the West inherited a *justifiable* sense of guilt that was suppressed or obscured through its transfer to an *unjustifiable* sense of guilt over the original colonial episodes. Such attitudes were furthered by a fatalistic acceptance of the outcome, and an aversion to criticism of any kind of ex-colonial or other overseas peoples who may have formed a grudge against Western influences.

Secondly, in the post-War period an intensive spirit of internationalism has arisen as a natural reaction against the evils of 1930s nationalism that culminated in the most destructive conflict in history. But this spirit of internationalism undermined all the positive bonding mechanisms of nationalism, essential for maintaining the cultural and economic integrity of a people. In other words, leading commentators forgot to differentiate between malign or negative or self-enclosed forms of nationalism, with those that are socially benign in unifying all sectors of the community, and in addition, towards a positive cosmopolitan outlook.

It is only now, in recent years, that these values are being restored to recognition in the face of major crises of international federations in failing to recognise the specific needs of nation states. Until the present time history has demonstrated that democracy as a form of government[9] is only workable within the nation state. Federations based on a general sympathy or alliance may remain stable, but as soon as they overreach themselves through encroaching on the business of overall government, they quarrel internally before falling apart.

Thirdly, the influence of cultural (as contrasted with political) Marxism that is now a leading influence in universities worldwide has advanced the interests of internationalism whilst attacking the concept of national identity in any way it can. Cultural Marxism is in close alliance with the liberal thinking of the far left, but both are now long divorced from popular thinking or the instincts of the majority. The cultural Marxism of academics is the main proponent of *political correctness*, with all its self-censorship, but it otherwise remains an arid soil for constructive political thought.

For all the above reasons, there is now a timidity amongst the majority in the face of external threats – i.e., a timidity in fear of causing offence. This allows a free rein for Muslims to behave as they wish irrespective of the anxieties of their host countries. In a democratic and peaceful society of well-meaning people the individual should be free to dress in any way he chooses, irrespective of eccentricity or the ridicule he may bring on himself. This is a natural right as any other. But such a right is called into question in the case of Muslims.

---

[9] See Chapter 4 of my book, *The Democratic Imperative*, in presenting the arguments for this.

When tens of thousands, or possibly, even hundreds of thousands, on the London Underground are daily put under the anxiety of ever completing their journey alive at the sight of Muslims in their native dress boarding the train as commuters, the question arises as to the right of imposing such stress on the ordinary public. These alarming passengers have clearly repudiated the dress codes of their host peoples, either out of indifference for their feelings or contempt for Western traditions. I have noted the expressions of alarm amongst ordinary passengers as Muslims board the tube – particularly if they have backpacks – and every heavily veiled woman seems to remain a potential bomber.

As a commuter, not on a daily, but nonetheless, on a frequent basis, I am left clutching a bottle in fear of my life – and with good reason, as within a month of having written these lines, I travelled my frequent route on a line where the stabbing by a Muslim fanatic occurred. Moreover, the incident occurred at a station where I sometimes change trains. If readers are alarmed at what they might feel is the exaggerated timidity of someone who has travelled in bandit-infested territory in the course of promoting international trade (in North Yemen, for example) and never blinked at the thought of danger, my personal excuse is that with the advance of years, and a weakening physique, one loses the natural courage of earlier years. And I have no doubt that there are many, like myself, who are placed in a similar situation in the Underground.

Terrorist acts may be a rare occurrence but the terrorist experience is nonetheless very frequent indeed. Surely legislation is justified to diminish the fears of the peace-loving public. In the absence of such legislation, is it right that commuters should be forced into a heroic mould – maybe beyond the limits of their endurance? If legislation was enacted obliging Muslims to shave off their beards and moustaches, and adopt Western dress with no indication of Islamic influence, a great relaxation and comfort would be awarded passengers on the London Underground.

We are certainly indebted to the police and MI5 in preventing more terrorist attacks than there would otherwise have been, but there is a far greater need for more research in understanding the thought processes that lead to extremism. The noted columnist, Charles Moore, has written about the established UK Islamist organisations that whilst not promoting violence, nonetheless all "preach extremism which creates the mental space in which violence can breed." He writes, "Islamism validates resentment. Its emotional appeal is like that of Communism and Fascism, but stronger, because it promises heaven to those who commit to its violent acts on earth." In supporting the arguments behind the central thesis of this book, he concludes by saying, "Ultimately, the capacity of a civilisation to resist those who hate it depends on its self-belief. In Europe, this was expressed in what was called Christendom, enriched by the ideas of the Enlightenment."[10]

Meanwhile, Prince Charles at a Sandhurst passing out parade for senior cadets in December 2015, delivered the following apt words of warning and advice of relevance to military defence: "You are receiving your commissions as officers at a moment when the profession of arms is moving into uncharted waters. Pillars of the international order are under challenge as never before in my lifetime. At the same time, a cult of death and destruction is defiling ancient lands and seducing and frightening numbers of lost young people. In the face of such challenges, Britain's traditional qualities – fair play, civility, a sense of humour in adversity – remains as precious as they've ever been."

2) Islam and the curbing of Free Speech throughout our Universities

The curbing of free speech in places of learning is probably the greatest internal danger that can confront any civilisation. The ossification of learning, or its gradual diminution, or its relapse into meaningless pedantry, are all symptoms of slow cultural

---

[10] Quotations taken from Charles Moore's article, "We could better tackle Islamism if we had greater cultural confidence," *The Daily Telegraph*, 12th December 2015.

decline, but censorship, howsoever embarked upon, or for whatever reason, is invariably a fast track to civilisation's ruin.

Leading academics in Britain and elsewhere are now maintaining that free speech is being curtailed in universities as never before. It is being imposed from three directions: firstly, through government anti-terrorism legislation under the label of Prevent; secondly, through university authorities, primarily with the aim of adhering to the principles of political correctness, or in preventing what they anticipate might lead to a breach of the peace; and thirdly, through student bodies for every conceivable reason of objection. As with many things, censorship becomes a self-fulfilling habit, and as it flexes its muscles, it needs to feed on ever more spheres of prohibition.

It is necessary, however, to trace its origin. It did not appear out of a vacuum. During the Cold War period the curtailing of free speech was promoted by the intellectual forces of Communism, both overtly and covertly, certainly until the Hungarian uprising in 1956, and thereafter it was promoted by Marxism and the far left – i.e., by Marxists and crypto-Marxists until around the fall of the Berlin Wall in 1989. Their methods usually took the form of aggressive meetings, the ridiculing of those with whom they disagreed, and occasionally, threats against academics to whom they took a dislike. Their success in crushing controversy was limited by the strength of opposing opinions.

Following an interregnum in the nature of political controversy in academic circles, everything had changed by the start of the new millennium. I have already noted the huge scale in the financing of Islam by Saudi Arabia and the other Gulf States in an earlier chapter. Their attack on universities worldwide, particularly in the developed economies, was part of the great strategy of the oil producing countries to Islamise the planet. The financial resources invested for this purpose dwarfed anything attempted by Moscow and the East bloc throughout the Cold War period. The Saudis and their allies attempted a low profile in promoting their campaign, but their expenditure was so great that they could hardly remain unnoticed for long. The university authorities, meanwhile, were in two minds about the situation: grateful for the generosity of funding, but embarrassed by the underlying purpose for such expenditure. Their natural response in such circumstances was therefore a quiet discretion.

The empowered Islamic students were raucous and demanding, one moment expressing their religiosity and extending friendly gestures in proselytising amongst the "infidels;" and the next in raising an angry protest against "discrimination" and the withholding of privileges to which they claimed a right. At this point the university authorities were forced to take a closer look at the problem, and quickly realised they were trapped in an un-resolvable situation. There was no precedent for the dilemma that was developing beneath their feet.

If the university authorities initiated measures specifically against the Islamic community that would not only be interpreted as "discrimination" but unfair, and against the principles of both "equality" and "democracy." Hence such a course of action was closed. The only alternative was to cast a wider net, so that the minnows would be caught alongside the whales, and in this way no accusations of "discrimination" could be made as all were involved as equals. This entailed clever bureaucratic manoeuvring, or the skilled formulation of "neutral" rules and regulations so designed as not to arouse offence from any direction. Their declared purpose was to safeguard the sensibilities of every conceivable minority from the risk of offending, through further promoting the already established principles of political correctness.

By this means the possibility of malfeasance became an ever-expanding cause of accusation, so that the basis of wrongdoing changed from one day to the next, and even those amongst the highest echelons of academia might unknowingly, or through accident, overstep the mark to the ruin of their reputations or even their careers. None of this could be achieved without the curbing of free speech, but as the motive for such regulations stemmed from benevolence or the demand for courtesy, no one was prepared to raise a voice in protest for fear of being tarnished as an anti-social, unpleasant, or malignant personality – if not something worse through the inventiveness of the political vocabulary.

Such restrictions motivated by fear and the need to balance commonsense against the absurd rather than the intentional attempt to oppress, led inevitably to regulations that were ludicrously incomprehensible – and not only in Britain, but in universities worldwide. The following are some of the more remarkable examples:- University of Manchester: two speakers, Julie Bindel, a radical feminist, and Milo Yiannoppoulos, a right wing blogger, were banned from a debate on free speech as it was alleged their views might encourage hatred; Harvard University: banned the title of "House master" because students complained it had overtones of slavery; University of East Anglia: students given free sombrero hats by a local Tex-Mex restaurant were asked not to wear them on campus as they contravened "strict cultural appropriation rules." The students union explained that, "Discriminatory or stereotypical language or imagery towards any group or individual based on characteristics will not be permitted as part of our advertising;" University of York: decided to ban an International Men's Day event because of complaints from students and staff. Opponents argued that such an event would have an "adverse impact on the equality of men;" University of Ottawa: banned a yoga class designed to include disabled students as the practice was taken from a culture "that experienced oppression, cultural genocide and diasporas due to colonialism and Western supremacy," viz., India; Oxford University: the university's union decided to ban the magazine, *No Offence*, whose aim was to promote free speech and invite debate from the Freshers' Fair, because some might find it offensive; and Cambridge University: the well-known historian, David Starkey, was dropped from a major promotional video because of his allegedly racist views.

When this intolerance and absurdity could no longer be endured by a group of eleven teaching academics from different institutions of learning, they decided to send a letter to the national press under the heading of *Student Censorship*. Under the leadership of Frank Furedi, professor of sociology at the University of Canterbury, of Prof. Dennis Hayes, and Maryam Namazie, a prominent human rights campaigner who initially was banned from speaking at Warwick University because of her atheism which it was feared might incite hatred on the campus, the following letter was published in the *Daily Telegraph* on 19th December 2015:-

"Sir. – At British universities, freedom of speech is being curtailed as never before. The Government's anti-terrorism legislation, known as Prevent, imposes restrictions on who can and cannot speak on campus and forces academics to police students and each other. At the same time, the list of speakers banned from unions by students is growing, and even banned artefacts: from pop songs to sombreros.

"With the rise of tuition fees, universities see students as customers. They face growing pressures to give students what they want. In turn, many of the most vocal students feel they have a right to demand protection from images, words and ideas that offend them.

"A small but vocal minority of student activists is arguing that universities need to be turned into 'safe places.' This represents an attempt to immunise academic life from the intellectual challenge of debating conflicting views. Banning speakers from campus is not new; there has never been a golden age of free speech at universities. Two things, however, are new: the number of bans being enacted has risen, and the targets are much more nebulous.

"Few academics challenge censorship from students. It is important that more do, because a culture that restricts the free exchange of ideas leaves people afraid to express their views in case they may be misinterpreted. This risks destroying the very fabric of democracy.

"An open and democratic society requires people to have the courage to argue against ideas they disagree with or even find offensive. At the moment there is a real risk that students are not given opportunities to engage in such debate.

"We call on academics and vice chancellors to take a much stronger stance against all forms of censorship. Students who are offended by opposing views are perhaps not yet ready to be at university."

In the above letter it will be noted that there is not a single reference to Islam or Muslims, and yet in every line of the letter there breathes the Islamic presence. If anyone peruses the notice boards of those colleges in central London, e.g., the UCL, the LSE, or King's College, or Imperial College in Kensington, or Queen Mary's in Mile End, etc., it will be found that the overwhelming majority on any one subject will either be advertisements of Islamic associations of one kind or another, or else notices announcing urgent Islamic meetings to protest against this or that.

Some years ago most colleges stipulated that all notices for posting on boards needed to go through the college office for approval before awaiting available space, but that does not prevent the unauthorised posting of notices. Appointed college officials will occasionally inspect boards and remove those notices without the approval stamp, but this has little impact on the energetic activity of Muslims in replacing those that have been torn down. There is nothing that deters the Muslim in promoting his own faith in any way he can.

The question may well be asked, not which country in the world exerts the greatest intellectual influence on institutions of learning, but rather which country exerts the greatest *power* over the universities of the world? It is certainly not America – and Russia long ago lost any claim to such an exalted status. And neither is it China. The prize for such an exalted position belongs to one country only, and it must be awarded to Saudi Arabia.

In an earlier chapter we showed how Saudi Arabia is the source for almost all Islamic terrorist groups on our planet – even those against which she is now obliged to fight for her existence. Saudi Arabia's power over the major universities of the world is her just reward for the gargantuan investments she has made for that very purpose. But is she prepared to acknowledge that power? I suspect she is disturbed by feelings of embarrassment. She would prefer to adopt a lower profile. The power has come too soon for the effective exploitation for a useful end.

CHAPTER 9
Islam at War with Christianity

"To be furious in religion is to be irreligiously religious."

William Penn, *Fruits of Solitude*

3) The threats against Christianity

The abstention from religion of any kind at the present day by the majority, in what we have described as the civilised world, is probably in greater part due to disgust at witnessing the fanaticism and horrors of fundamentalism than any natural inclination towards agnosticism. It may be even less due to the barren, negative and atheistic mindset of contemporary humanism (common amongst some intellectuals), a frame of mind that should not be confused with the creative Humanism of the Renaissance period that rejected medieval Scholasticism with its theological bias.

It may further be assumed that the majority referred to above feel little affinity with those faith leaders intent on ridding public life of Christianity – in fact they may be outraged at the suggestion. And yet it is something that calls for an explanation. In early December 2015, within three weeks of the Christmas festival, a report was published following a two-year commission chaired by the former senior judge, Baroness Butler-Sloss, involving leading religious leaders of most faiths, openly advocating that public life be systematically de-Christianised. Patrons behind the Commission included Rowan Williams, the former Archbishop of Canterbury, Lord Woolf, the former Lord Chief Justice, and Sir Iqbal Sacranie, the former General Secretary of the Muslim Council of Britain.

The report argued that in view of the decline of church-going and the rise of Islam and other beliefs, a "new settlement" was called for religion in the UK giving more official influence to non-Christian faiths. The report further argued that: a) Faith schools are "socially divisive" and selection of children on the basis of their beliefs should be phased out; b) The number of

Church of England bishops in the Lords should be replaced with imams, rabbis and other non-Christian clerics as well as evangelical pastors; c) Acts of worship in school assemblies needed to be abolished and replaced with "a time for reflection;" d) The Coronation service for the next monarch to be overhauled to include other faiths; and, e) Thought for the Day on BBC Radio 4's *Today* programme to include non-religious addresses – which in fact it already does, and would be known to the Commission members had they regularly listened to the programme.

Undoubtedly, the most controversial recommendation of the report was the call for a rethink of anti-terror policy, permitting students to voice radical views on campus without fear of being reported to the security services. It then implied that recognition should be given to Sharia law by recommending new protection for women in their courts and those of other religious tribunals.

Before reporting on the immediate response to Baroness Butler-Sloss's report, it may be more worthwhile to give it some analysis. The proposed restrictions on free choice or the opportunity for alternative systems to flourish alongside each other, as would result from the abolition of faith schools, or the ending of acts of worship in school assemblies, may be passed over without comment. Of more interest are the circumstances and pressures under which the Commission operated.

Clearly the participants came to the Commission with widely diverse and even uncompromising views. Collective decisions needed to be reached that were "fair" and satisfactory to all present, as otherwise the task could never have been completed. As with any collection of animals, irrespective of whether they be hens or humans, it was inevitable that the strongest or more determined would emerge triumphant. But such an outcome does not mean, in objective terms, that the best decisions are thereby necessarily reached.

Those participants who come to such a meeting with a totally uncompromising attitude, but nonetheless exude a certain charm and persuasiveness will usually win the day. And that is why it is a futile exercise in bringing extreme opposites together in the hope of a happy outcome. The forces of Islam emerged victorious with the presentation of the report's findings to the public. They could not have hoped for a better triumph. By a process of attrition, step-by-step, they were undermining the Christian religion by dismantling its long established institutional functions.

There is something more that must be said on the rigidity of those whose judgement may never be changed, i.e., the fanatics who keep an enemy in view for its eventual destruction. Islam is by no means unique in this respect. Marxists present the classic example. It is impossible to have an open and honest discussion with Marxists, as from the time of their founder they always prevaricate and emerge, in their own opinion, the only possible victor in any discussion. If they lose an argument on purely factual grounds, they may have the courtesy to acknowledge defeat, but as soon as your back is turned, they will maintain their original position as if no discussion had taken place.

The acrimony of Marxism from its beginnings is accountable to the metaphysics of dialectical materialism, or the technique of promoting revolution, and that the means is always justified by the end. Marxism is in itself essentially dishonest as the fallibility of the system is found in the fact that its predictions do not meet the reality of the everyday world. Those who attempted to negotiate with Hitler were no less deluded than those who hoped for a happy outcome through a dialogue with Marxists. Hitler had his enemies in sight, and no charm on either side was going to detract him from his single purpose.

Islam is no less determined in its single purpose than the Nazis or Communists. Its ideology is the One God, and its enemy are the infidels or all non-Muslims, and its political purpose is the achievement of a worldwide Caliphate. There is something pitiable about those religious leaders, together with its minority of non-believers, comprising Baroness Butler-Sloss's Commission. The clergy are always full of good intentions and philanthropic purpose, but at the best of times, they tend to have a feeble grasp of practicalities or *Realpolitik*.

One recollects their role during the height of the Cold War through CND and similar peace-loving organisations and the absurdity of the idea of dialogue with Soviet diplomats and politicians. I have no doubt that the Soviets exuded charm and deferred with every act of courtesy to these men in holy orders, and that the latter were suitably seduced and drawn along to all kinds of curious compromises that fed back to the general public as well as to the political establishment. If any influence was exerted through these absurd discussions it was only likely to have weakened resolve in confronting Communist expansionism.

Equally absurd and contemptible are the innumerable groups in our own time supposedly promoting greater harmony between the Christian churches and Islam. It may be that those who are moved and live by the principle of Revelation are quintessentially unfitted for the practical responsibility of managing the affairs of the world. Muslims, too, believe in Revelation, but they are built in a tougher mould than their Christian counterparts. The Christian clergy, as with the majority in the Western world, tend to be yielding to the wishes of those beyond their own frontiers. They are soft and tolerant by contrast with Muslims who are intolerant and rigid in their convictions. Hence in a conference mode Christians will tend to be trusting, good-natured, optimistic and gullible in contrast to Muslims who will be indomitable, realistic, and suspicious behind a friendly mask. To imagine that a dialogue between two such rivals is at the same time a dialogue between equals, or to anticipate that the outcome of such a dialogue may resolve successfully substantive issues for the longer term, is just ridiculous. It is rather as if a sheep was to entire into a dialogue with a wolf as to whether or not it should be eaten.

As may be anticipated, Baroness Butler-Sloss's report aroused outrage in the public sphere. The Church of England condemned the report as a "sad waste" and that it had "fallen captive to liberal rationalism." A spokesman further added, "The report is dominated by the old-fashioned view that traditional religion is declining in importance and that non-adherence to a religion is the same as humanism or secularism." Meanwhile, a source close to the Education Secretary, Nicky Morgan, described the recommendations on faith schools as, "ridiculous," adding that, "Nicky is one of the biggest champions of faith schools and anyone who thinks she is going to pay attention to these ridiculous recommendations is sorely misguided."

Nonetheless, it does not mean that this vigorous response from the C. of E. or the government will necessarily prevail for the longer term. As too often happens on the political scene, one day there is denial, and on the next, to the surprise of all, there is surrender. It is the drip-drip of attrition rather than rhetoric that always wins in the end.

If the above is an example of the war of attrition against long-established Christian institutions, the following illustrates how Christianity may become an accidental victim of anti-radicalisation measures. In November 2015 a consultation paper was published by the Department for Education which alarmed Christian groups on account of plans that could unwittingly turn the Oftsed watchdog into a "state regulator of religion." In a letter sent by the Christian Institute to the Education Secretary, it was argued that unless steps are taken to limit such plans, they would represent an "unprecedented attack on freedom of religion in this country." At the same time, the Evangelical Alliance, representing two million practising British Christians, claimed it risked the "wholesale nationalisation of youth work and the indirect state regulation of private religious practice."

The furore arose from proposals following warnings of the Prime Minister, David Cameron, over the minority of Muslim madrassas and other groups where children have their "heads filled with poison and their hearts filled with hate." The alarm was originally raised through an Ofsted inspection and the exposure of the "Trojan horse" affair, and the subsequent decision to include "British values" within the remit of future tests and as to whether or not "tolerance" and "democracy" were also taught.

It was envisaged that the new plans would be applicable to any institution providing "tuition, training or instruction" to under 19s for more than six hours a week. Inspectors would be on the lookout for "undesirable teaching," and anyone judged to be promoting "extremism" would be banned from "working with children." The summary of the criticism of the above proposals was made by Colin Hart of the Christian Institute when he said, "The idea of having an Ofsted inspector sitting in on your church youth group or Sunday school to see if you are an extremist is, I have to say, highly offensive. It would represent an unprecedented attack on freedom of religion in our country."

Colin Hart's remarks are, of course, fully justified. Once again, the problem arises from a misplaced attempt at "fairness," or the fear of giving offence when the latter might necessarily be called for. It is a form of dishonesty, stemming from cowardice that worsens all-round good relationships within the community. For the sake of resolving the problem at the core, rather than enlarging it to irritate the broader population, it would have been better to legislate for the Muslim community alone, as they alone and no others were responsible for the original offence. This may be taking the bull by the horns, but sometimes justice and fairness demands such a course of action.

The outrages on a human minority, inflicted by Muslims, I leave to this final section on the threats against Christianity – which more correctly might be entitled, The Persecution of Christianity. At a reception in Westminster hosted by Cardinal Vincent Nichols, Archbishop of Westminster, held for Middle East Christians, and attended by the Prince of Wales on 17th December 2015, the Archbishop pointed out that the government's plan to resettle 20,000 Syrian refugees in the UK risked "discriminating" against Christians. This did not arise through any fault of the British government, but through the fact that the UNHCR rules forbids deliberate discrimination on the basis of religion.

Cardinal Nichols explained that few, if any, Christian families fleeing the Islamic State of Iraq and the Levant militants would be offered sanctuary in the UK as the aid scheme is UN-led and separate from the church-run centres where most of the persecuted Christians are concentrated. He added that this was an "unintended consequence" of the plan but a "point of deep concern for Catholic and Orthodox and other Christian churches with a stake in the region." The Prince recounted the atrocious treatment of Christians in the Middle East and other regions, including torture, beheadings and even young people being buried alive.

By comparison with Islamic refugees the Christians are doubly disadvantaged: firstly, because they are entangled in an internecine war not of their own making; and secondly, because as a distinctive minority with a different faith, they are the victims of a vicious persecution. If justice is to prevail it would only be right if Britain were to cooperate with her allies in the Middle East (including Russia which has a vested interest in view of the many Orthodox believers in the region), in rescuing the Christians from further harm before any additional Muslims are allowed to enter any part of Europe.

Whilst Muslims must accept the moral blame for the consequences of their *enthusiasm*, excess zealotry, fanaticism – call it what you will – that has brought bloodshed to their peoples, the Christians have remained a moderate and peace-loving people who have never sought to hurt their neighbours. Surely the Christian refugees should be welcomed to Europe with the promise of their eventual integration, rather than the Muslims who will forever remain apart and may be a source of turbulence and terror for the future.

Only now are Christian leaders beginning to strike back seriously in defence of their faith against the Islamic onslaught. And this is in the light of persecution rather than mere threats, and they may be cited as under:- a) Brunei has recently issued a notification that anyone publicly celebrating Christmas will be subject to up to five years imprisonment, and that a fine of $20,000 will be imposed on those performing any ceremony contrary to Sharia law. This wide-ranging penal code would include singing religious songs, sending festive greetings, or putting up Christmas trees, crosses or candles. b) In 2013 Somalia's leading clerics had already issued a similar edict, that was recently reiterated by the Religious Affairs Minister, Sheikh Mohamed Khayron, that "all events related to Christmas and new year celebrations are contrary to Islamic culture," adding that they could, "damage the faith of the Muslim community," and risk attracting terrorist attacks from Al Shabaab.

c) In Sudan (as in other Islamic countries) apostasy is punished by death, and suspects have been tortured by the authorities. d) In Saudi Arabia, under the new terrorism law, criticism of the government's interpretation of Islam is punishable by a prison term ranging between 3 and 20 years. e) In Iran during 2015 the authorities have raided several church services, imprisoning worshippers and church leaders, particularly evangelical converts. f) In Uzbekistan the government brands evangelical Protestants and Jehovah's Witnesses as "extremists," and they face fines, detention and arrest. g) In Burma in January 2015 two Kachin Christian women volunteering as teachers with the Kachin Baptist Convention were raped and murdered in Shan state, allegedly by the Burmese army.

According to the Catholic University of Notre Dame in Paris, 80% "of all acts of religious discrimination in the world" are inflicted against Christians. The situation is most acute in the Middle East, which is home to the oldest Christian communities in the world. At a conference in Rome in December 2015, Patriarch Ignatius Youssef III Younan, declared that, "Middle East Christians have been forgotten, abandoned, even betrayed by the Western countries."

In response to the above and other abuses, the Bishop of Leeds, Nick Baines, wrote a percipient letter under the banner of the Thunderer, published in *The Times* on Christmas Eve 2015, the greater part of which is reproduced below:-

Christians are the most persecuted of all world faiths

"Religious special pleading is rarely convincing or attractive. Overblown complaints about being picked on run the danger of diminishing or trivialising genuine suffering. So it is remarkable that when Christians are targeted for the most appalling persecution, politicians and media commentators find it difficult to name it for what it is. To identify the persecution of Christians is not to diminish the suffering of others.

"It is reckoned that Christians represent the most persecuted people on earth in the 21st century. And we are not talking here of a bit of ridicule or silly marginalisation. We are talking about men, women and children being singled out because of their Christian faith or identity and put to an unimaginably cruel death. Or being driven out of home, away from livelihood, deprived of identity and dignity. Or, for women and girls being forced into sexual slavery and subjected to rape-at-will. …

"The specific nature of anti-Christian persecution in many parts of the world (Nigeria, say, or Pakistan) make it difficult to identify a single solution; but the complexity or ubiquity of the phenomenon should not lead to embarrassed silence on the part of the largely religiously illiterate Western intelligentsia. Where Christians are being persecuted, the word should be used without embarrassment."

On Christmas day 2015, both Pope Francis and the Archbishop of Canterbury, Justin Welby, amongst many other church leaders in their sermons, drew attention to the persecution of Christians worldwide. The Most Rev. Justin Welby, who heads the world's 85 million Anglicans, noted in his sermon that the terrorism of Isis is an ultimate threat, "Confident that these are the last days, using force and indescribable cruelty (Isis) seem to welcome all opposition, certain that the warfare unleashed confirms that these are indeed the end times. … They hate difference, whether it is Muslims who think differently, Yazidis or Christians, and because of them the Christians face elimination in the very region in which Christian faith began. This apocalypse is defined by themselves and heralded only by the angel of death. To all who have been or are being dehumanised by the tyranny and cruelty of a Herod or an Isis, a Herod of today, God's judgement comes as good news, because it promises justice."

It would be apt to conclude this chapter with the projected evidence [11] for the decline of Christianity in the Middle East resulting from the persecution and massacres inflicted by the Muslim majority:-

	1970	2020
Syria	9.7%	4.1%
Jordan	5%	2.3%
Iraq	3.7%	1.2%
Egypt	17%	9%
Lebanon	62.3%	33.5%
Israel	2.8%	2.1%
Palestine	4.7%	1.2%
Turkey	0.8%	0.2%

---

[11]   Figures taken from *The Times*, 26th December 2015.

CHAPTER 10

The West's Response to the Breakdown of Law and Order

"It is right to be religious, but one should shun religiosity."
(Religentem esse oportit; religiosus ne funs.)

Publius Negidius Figulus, *Commentatiorum Grammaticorum*,
Bk. XI.

4) The failure of the police to act against Islamic threats

Davig Cameron was right when he criticised Donald Trump, the Republican candidate for the US Presidency, for casting aspersions on the integrity of the British police, and for portraying a grossly exaggerated picture of their timidity in the face of Islamic threats. And yet Donald Trump must be acknowledged for identifying a long-lasting source of anxiety amongst the British public over a concern that has been repressed as a matter for debate.

It is wrong that the public should be placed in a situation of fear due to the want of vigour by the custodians of the law. It is also understandable that there is a reluctance to question the effectiveness of those appointed to protect our security and keep order in the streets. The problem arises from a cause already touched upon many times in this book, viz., the fear of accusation in discriminating against a minority, and especially if a racial slant may falsely be interpreted.

The Race Relations Act, or rather matters pertaining to it, is abused a thousand times a day. In reality lawbreaking is *never* a racial issue, but it is falsely cast in such a mould whenever a specific minority happens to be prone to committing certain offences. Whilst on the one hand it is highly regrettable when those of a certain race are picked-upon for stop and search, on the other hand, in present circumstances, it remains an unfortunate necessity if the police are to be effective, and it calls for a two-way understanding and an exchange of courtesies when it transpires that the outcome is negative. If the police may be exonerated from accusations of impropriety in the above situations, providing civility is shown to those who are mistakenly suspected of wrongdoing, there are other situations when the police clearly betray a timidity for fear of upsetting better race relations.

This occurs with Muslims in a variety of lawbreaking incidents. Their loud-mouthed cries of "discrimination," together with the help of friends in powerful places, affords them considerable protection, particularly when the wrongdoing exists on a borderline that is crossed and re-crossed. It would be unjust to suggest that timidity alone was responsible for police reluctance in taking effective action, for not only is there the question of the complexity of the law, but more significantly, the question of how best to secure sound evidence in preparing charges that will stick.

A recent study by Her Majesty's Inspectors of Constabulary has revealed that police investigating "honour" crimes have been accused of putting victims at risk by inadvertently tipping off perpetrators about investigations at a sensitive early stage. The report alleged that police were sometimes "speaking with the wrong people" on receiving information about honour violence or female genital mutilation. Honour crimes are an increasingly common occurrence with 11,000 cases reported to the police between 2010 and 2014. Researchers interviewed 50 victims for the study: including 10 from Somalia, 9 from India, and 8 from Pakistan. The study maintained that, "overall we found that the need to speak with the right people to build intelligence, and the risk to victims of speaking with the wrong people, was not always well understood by police officers and staff. The right people are not necessarily faith and community leaders, who may sometimes be the very people promoting or supporting harmful practices in the name of honour."

For example, one victim told researchers that when police arrived at her home at the start of an investigation her mother-in-law was in the room and her husband was upstairs. She made it clear to the police that she could not possibly talk with them in the home. It was no surprise, therefore, that the Inspectorate of

Constabulary found that only 3 out of 43 police forces were adequately prepared to deal with honour crimes. It was also revealed that out of 1,200 victims of forced marriage who made referrals to the Foreign Office's Forced Marriage Unit in 2014 only 80 cases were referred to prosecutors. Between 2012 and the close of 2015, 15 female genital mutilation cases had been referred by police to the Crown Prosecution Service with no further action taken in 14 of those, whilst the other resulted in acquittal.

Most shocking to the peoples of the civilised world is the contempt that Muslims have for women and the oppression to which they are subjected. All women are placed legally (i.e. according to Islamic law) under the tutelage of a male guardian, being responsible for their behaviour and especially for safeguarding their moral reputation. If the guardian is not a father or husband, it may be an uncle or even a younger brother who may still be in his teenage years. No younger woman may leave the house without the authority of the guardian, and never unaccompanied. As soon as a woman approaches old age, which in the Islamic world is considered around 40+, and has grown sufficiently unattractive and obese, she is judged sufficiently safe and discreet to be relatively independent in public places to engage in such activities as selling fruit or gewgaws laid out on a carpet in the street.

Younger women are usually accompanied by groups of elders when leaving the home. Those who recollect the story, in an earlier chapter of this book, of the women fighting to board the back of a bus, may be interested to know that I was in the company of my sponsor when this scene was witnessed. His moral comment on the disgraceful episode was, "That's what happens when you allow women out of the house." He then went on to explain that the men in his family never allowed their womenfolk to leave the home unaccompanied by men, and that the latter took full responsibility for all household shopping. Whilst one husband shopped for meat, another bought the vegetables, whilst another attended to toiletries. In this way they "protected" their women from the "cruel realities" of the outside world.

The above paragraphs have been included as an essential guide to understanding Islamic (usually Pakistani) attitudes of Muslim men towards Western women and what we describe as "under age" girls. The assumption of Muslims that all Westerners are incontinent arises through the self-isolation of their communities and reluctance to integrate within the host community, whilst their proclivity for under-age girls is accountable to the fact that their own women marry at the age of 14 or even as young as 12. These cultural misconceptions, of course, are no excuse for lawbreaking. The police have been particularly lax in their willingness to prosecute Muslims for their systematic grooming, seduction, raping, and induction into prostitution of Western women and under-age girls.

This reluctance has not occurred through deference to cultural differences but rather through the obsessive fear of appearing racist or being publicly exposed to such an accusation. This reluctance is furthered by the large number of Muslim councillors and mayors now found in local authorities throughout the UK, for these people are a significant influence on police behaviour. Meanwhile, vote-rigging and other forms of political corruption in local government by the Muslim community has already been exposed in the courts.

The greatest difficulty confronting the police is the silence or non-compliance of the Islamic community in cooperating with anti-extremism measures. This is the most appalling aspect of Islamic terrorism today, for it makes those who could be most helpful in resolving the problem, complicit by default in assisting the evil. It allows for a situation whereby no Muslim is above suspicion. The international *Prevent* programme, being part of the counter-terrorism strategy set-up in the wake of 9/11, is now under direct attack by Muslim leaders on the grounds that it is, "racist or akin to a McCarthyite witch-hunt where community members are encouraged to shop their neighbours or even school friends to the police."

In December 2015 the Waltham Forest Council of Mosques, representing tens of thousands of East London Muslims, announced a boycott of Prevent, whilst Muslim leaders in nearby Newham, warned that it is "spying on our young people." Figures from the National Police Chiefs Council reveal that of the 3,288 referrals to the Prevent programme in the first half of 2015, only 280 or 8.6% came from the Islamic community, and their family, friends and faith leaders. Another 2,180 referrals were from public bodies outside policing, such as schools, social services and the health sector. The remainder came from the police and within prisons.[12]

If the British police may be accused of being fearful in the face of Muslim lawbreaking, the timidity of the German police has been even more shocking in its extent. When female revellers were sexually attacked and robbed on New Year's Eve in Cologne by up to 1,000 Muslim men described as being of North African or Middle Eastern appearance, the authorities attempted a complete publicity shutdown on the episode. Some days after the event, a 32-year old named Ilse, exclaimed that, "something terrible took place here, but it's as if it never occurred. I was there in the chaos and terror doing nothing. And now we are expected to say nothing? Just because the perpetrators were immigrants? This is another attack on women: first on our bodies, now on our rights."

A 26-year old woman added, "It was terrifying. I got separated from my boyfriend and as they were pulling at my clothes I thought I would be raped right there in public. I screamed for help but everywhere I looked the same thing was happening; attack and robbery. But just women! They targeted us because we were women." It was alleged that victims suffered permanent burns as men threw fireworks into the crowd to cause fear and confusion. A father related how he watched helplessly, clutching his baby son as his partner and 15-year old daughter were swept away and mauled by men thrusting hands inside their jeans and underwear. In the immediate aftermath,

---

[12] Facts taken from Fiona Hamilton's report in *The Times*, on 26th December 2015.

whilst one major TV network chose not to report the story, the press stated categorically that, "there was no evidence refugees were among the assailants," even though such a contention was known to be false from the start, and despite the fact that over 170 women came forward in reporting assault – 113 being for sexual assault, an unspecified number of robberies, and two cases of rape.

Another witness, 24-year old, Isabella Prodam, burst out, "I would deport the lot of them. New Year's Eve was a nightmare. These men bring with them African values that have no place in Europe; they treat women like objects, without respect. I lived in Africa for three years and when I did, I obeyed their customs. They must do the same or go home." When the Mayor of Cologne, Henrietta Reker, advised women to protect themselves from future attack by keeping "more than an arm's length away" from strangers, an 18-year old, Lena Reimer, outraged by this victim-blaming, retorted, "I feel angry that women are being expected to change their behaviour. I have nothing against refugees. ... but women are the victims here yet it is our freedom that is being curtailed."[13] It should also be noted that similar attacks were subsequently reported from Bielefeld, Hamburg, Frankfurt and Berlin.

The outcome of the Cologne episode was that Rolf Jäger, the Interior Minister of North Rhine-Westphalia, suspended Wolfgang Albers, the police chief of Cologne, from further duties, because of his mishandling of the situation. In the words of Rolf Jäger, this was, "necessary to regain the public's trust. The Cologne police now have the vital task of investigating the events of New Year's Eve. People rightly want to know what happened, who the perpetrators were and how such incidents can be prevented in the future." A complaisant Wolfgang Albers meanwhile commented, "It's part of my job to take responsibility in difficult times. The facts need to be thoroughly reviewed. The public debate about my person can only obstruct and delay this important work."

---

[13] As reported by Judith Woods under the heading of "First Person" in the *Daily Telegraph*, 9th January 2016.

Reports of similar assaults on women by asylum seekers across northern Europe soon emerged in the wake of the Cologne outrages: in Finland three asylum seekers had been arrested following plans to harass women in Helsinki, described by Ikka Koskimäki, the Deputy police chief of the city, as a "completely new phenomenon in Helsinki." In Sweden 15 women reported being sexually assaulted in Kalmar on New Year's Eve, and two asylum seekers had been arrested in connection with the crimes. In Switzerland, the Zürich police reported that six women had been sexually assaulted and robbed in cases "a little similar to those in Germany."[14]

In a penetrating article by Allison Pearson[15] in the *Daily Telegraph* on 8th January 2016, she reminded readers that the Cologne and subsequent sexual assault episodes were not a new phenomenon in Europe. She recollected how a group of drunken Libyan cadets stationed at RAF Bassingbourn ran amok in the centre of Cambridge in October 2014, sexually assaulting four women and raping one man. The rapists were jailed for 12 years apiece, and the gropers were given shorter terms and deported. The accused pleaded in their defence that they had not known that such behaviour was forbidden in England. Allison Pearson's comment was that, "This puts a liberal Western society, which values women's rights, and admits men from countries that don't, in a bit of a bind. It's difficult to raise the issue without being howled down by cries of *Islamophobia*. ... Sharia law shall not be imposed on us by stealth or cowardly accommodation with repellent thugs. ... I hope that I am wrong, but I fear that the gross mass attack on women in Cologne was not an isolated incident, but the first of many battles in a clash of civilisations."

An analysis of the facts and processes described in the above four sections will reveal that the Islamic community pose much more than a threat to Britain, and in the wider sphere, to

---

[14] As reported by Justin Huggler in the *Daily Telegraph*, 9th January 2016.
[15] *Rape is not a 'Cultural Misunderstanding.'*

world civilisation. They are already engaged in a war of attrition against an enemy that only offers appeasement in return. Their religious leaders urge that friendship should be avoided with the "infidels" and that contact should be kept to a minimum, and this ensures a necessary segregation for a desirable war-footing.

    Appeasement in the face of attrition inevitably generates conflict amongst the former. Differences in strategy do not create a multiplicity of choices, as might be thought, but rather the compounding of problems leading to paralysis. This was experienced by the Western democracies in 1930s Europe in challenging fascism, as it is experienced today in challenging an uncompromising Islam that is inherently undemocratic to its very core. The absolute obedience to a god whose commands are fully defined in holy script is totally incompatible with the demands of democracy in best serving the needs of the people. The unholy trinity of Freedom, Reason, and Knowledge, are all regarded as undesirable characteristics by the Wahabism that dominates contemporary Islam worldwide.

    When the police are accused of promoting "espionage" through the anti-radicalisation programme of Prevent, attempts are made by those with a softer heart to frustrate their efforts, and so to heighten the risk of terrorist attacks. When church leaders advocate the "partial introduction of Sharia law," they seem unaware of inserting the thinner end of a wedge. When the voice of a moderate Christianity, at peace with the idea of a changing and developing world, is confronted by the extremism of a fanatical religion, it cannot hope to maintain its balance or rightful position in the world. When a culture or civilisation loses the self-confidence for its overall superiority as the leading influence for the future of humankind, it has taken the first turn for its self-destruction. When cries of protest are made against free speech on grounds of "discrimination" or the nebulous abstractions of "political correctness," a dagger has been thrust into the heart of democracy. When all religions are muted or banned in educational establishments because one of their number happens to offer a terrorist threat, then the equality principle is turned into an act of tyranny.

Everything so far in this book has demonstrated the need for World Civilisation to formulate a constructive strategy to challenge the advance of Islamism. Such a cause is not merely to benefit non-Muslims, but more significantly, to advance the interests of Muslims as free human beings in a world of peace and justice. When we talk of the victims of terrorism, it should be noted that many times more Muslims have been slaughtered by their own people than they have slaughtered non-Muslims. Deaths resulting from the recent wars of the Middle East have for the most part been self-inflicted with a marginal impact by outsiders, and that resulting from purely philanthropic motives in ridding tyrants.

As we noted earlier in this book, over-population is the indirect cause for conflict in the Middle East, assisted by the injustice of the Palestinian situation; whilst the direct cause stems from what our sagacious 18th century ancestors contemptuously described as *enthusiasm*, or excess religiosity – being a disease of the mind that makes a virtue out of the most destructive evil. Regarding the indirect or base cause of conflict in the Middle East, biologists have long since observed that when any species of animal or insect reproduces itself in excess, there occurs a self-destructive psychosis culminating in a dramatic reduction of numbers. In the human species, which is conscious or reflective, this usually takes the form of warlike irrationality as manifested through a religiosity that disdains any attempt at intelligent explanation.

The tragedy of the Middle East situation is that it has over-spilled to threaten the civilisation of the world. Before attempting to resolve the underlying problem of Islam, it would first be useful to glance at the Western response in its several forms, both desirable and otherwise, to Islamic threats.

Islamic terrorism has at last – but only recently – brought a defensive response from governments and the media to the outrages of the past 15 or so years. As yet the response has tended to be superficial and instinctive rather than thoughtfully considered and intended for the longer term. Calls for the resumption of bombing in Syria or Iraq, whilst abstaining apprehensively from the idea of boots on the ground, may satisfy the urge for aggression or revenge, but is unlikely to contribute to a permanent settlement for the future. Hence the feelings of Jeremy Corbyn on the far left or Max Hastings on the centre right are probably justified in their agreement on this issue.

Following the Paris massacre in November 2015, the following month proved a busy time for the defenders of freedom. On 6th December, Pierre Grawegna, Luxembourg's Finance Minister, holding the presidency of the EU Council, declared that there was no other choice but to tear up budget rules and increase spending to stop future atrocities. He maintained that in these exceptional circumstances, governments needed to prioritise security over fiscal discipline and the so-called Stability and Growth Pact that limits budget deficits to 3% of gross domestic product.

On the same day, in touching on another aspect of the same problem, in an interview with *Bild am Sonntag*, the German Vice-Chancellor, Sigmar Gabriel, publicly accused Saudi Arabia of financing Islamic extremism in the West and warned that it must stop. He declared, "We have to make it clear to the Saudis that the time of looking away is over. ... Wahabi mosques all over the world are financed by Saudi Arabia. Many Islamists who are a threat to public safety come from these communities in Germany."

It is unusual for a Western leader to speak so directly against a supposedly "key Arab ally" of the West, but the above remarks were probably made in the light of King Salman's offer to build 200 mosques for Syrian refugees arriving in Germany – a gesture for which the King had already been widely criticised in the Republic. The Vice-Chancellor's intervention on this issue came only days after German intelligence issued a public warning that Saudi Arabia is at risk of becoming a major destabilising force in the Arab world.

It may be noted that this was not the first time the Vice-Chancellor had clashed with the Saudi Royal family, for on a trip to Riyadh earlier in the same year, he spoke out in support of Raif Badwi, the Saudi blogger sentenced to 1,000 lashes for allegedly "insulting Islam." On Friday 4th December the German parliament voted to deploy up to 1,200 military personnel to support international air strikes against Isil (Islamic State of Iraq and Levant), not for directly taking part in combat missions, but for providing reconnaissance flights and force protection.

On 18th December 2015, Britain (represented by George Osborne and Philip Hammond) together with her global allies met under the banner of the UN Security in New York, to discuss attacking Isil on five fronts. Firstly, this was concerned with countering the terror threat on the home front with a strategy to prevent attacks that leave no hiding place for the extremist ideology that feeds it. Secondly, diplomatic action to produce a political transition for a new Syria through negotiations between the Syrian opposition and the Assad regime. Thirdly, to continue humanitarian support to those fleeing the country, for which the British government had already allocated £1.1 billion, and a further billion to support post-conflict reconstruction and stabilisation. Fourthly, moves to be taken to challenge Daesh's propaganda, and to undermine its ideology and stop the flow of recruits to its deadly cause. And fifthly, the international financial system to be used to prevent Daesh from benefiting from its seizure of oilfields in the region.

Whilst diplomatic measures, as described above were initiated to combat terrorism, at the same time the intelligence services were stepping up their endeavours through the work of the immigration authorities. Migrants who wish to enter the UK will now undergo background checks that will include monitoring of their social media histories and any other online activities. Britain's counter-extremism strategy states: "We will make it more explicit that the criteria for exclusion on the grounds of unacceptable behaviour include past or current extremist activity, either here or overseas. Those who intend to travel to the UK should be clear about our expectations. We can already refuse to grant a visa to those whose presence in the UK is not conducive to the public good. We will ensure that more information on an individual's extremist behaviour is available to the officers making these visa decisions."

In America the Immigration Department has been criticised over reports it did not routinely consult social media during the vetting process for visa applications. Jeh Johnson, the American Homeland Security Secretary, stated, "We had policies in place regarding consulting social media which in my judgement, particularly in this current environment, were too restrictive. We in fact began to consult social media in connection with conferring various immigration benefits and we will be doing more of this." This prevarication seems to have reflected carelessness by the authorities, for Tashfeen Malik, who together with her husband, murdered 14 people in San Bernardino, California, early in December 2015, entered the US on a "Fiancée" visa, and it was later reported she had pledged her support for Jihadists in a private Facebook posting, although the FBI disputed those reports.

Since then the US has wisely strengthened the security of its borders. Donald Trump's appeal that no Muslims should be allowed into the US until the situation was somehow resolved was ignored as he lacked any real authority, but nonetheless, within a week or so, there was an outcry when apparently more than 20 British Muslim families were barred from entering America without any explanation for the decision. The Labour MPs Stella Creasy and Keith Vaz received complaints from constituents saying they had been turned back in the UK by US officials. Keith Vaz, the Labour Chairman of the Home Affairs Select Committee, issued a statement that "there are now a number of examples of British citizens who happen to be of the Muslim faith being refused entry to the USA without explanation. I will be writing to the US Ambassador seeking a full explanation and if this is not forthcoming I will recommend to the Committee that we can call him to give evidence." When the US Embassy was approached on the issue, they gave the standard reply that, "We do not comment on the details of individual cases."

Every country, of course, has the right to ban the entry of aliens for any reason it chooses. There is now a campaign, for example, to ban Donald Trump from entering Britain on the grounds of objecting to his free speech. With regard to the present issue, there are several facts to be noted. Firstly, America has far fewer Muslims per capita than any country in Western Europe, and although she has experienced her own several incidents of Islamic terrorism, she has looked on with horror at what has occurred in Europe. It is often the case that witnessing outrages from a distance exerts a greater impact than when they occur on one's own doorstep.

Secondly, through her own democratic choice America lives under the curse of a gun law situation that not only facilitates mass murder on a recurring basis but also possibly encourages it. Hence, to the American mind, the thought of a mix between Muslims and a liberal gun law is, either rightly or wrongly, so explosive and horrific, as to be intolerable. In view of such a mindset, it is therefore understandable, and perhaps desirable, that Muslims without a diplomatic status should be forbidden entry to the country until such time as the gun law is amended in satisfying the safety needs of the general public, or else, when Islamic people have undergone a sufficient level of reform and secularisation as no longer to be a threat to others.

The most alarming warning, during the busy month of December 2015, on the Islamic threat was possibly that of James Comey, the director of the FBI. On the 16th he stated that Isis had "revolutionised" terrorism and that the world faces a much more serious threat today than ever before. Speaking at a press conference in New York, he explained that the group's decentralised structure and use of social media to spread propaganda and incite attacks made it particularly difficult to combat, and that "Your parents' al-Qaeda was a very different model than the threat we face today." He said that the ability of Isil conspirators to use encrypted communications, and the constant threat of small-scale attacks worldwide brought new challenges to US law enforcement.

At the same time that James Comey was in New York, Jeh Johnson was in Washington, unveiling a new a system to alert the public to terrorist threats. He explained how the National Threat Advisory System would be revised so that the public would be alerted to "general developments or trends regarding threats of terrorism" through bulletins posted to the Homeland Security website. The first such bulletin, posted on 15th December, read as follows: "We are in a new phase in the global terrorist threat, which has implications on the homeland, particularly with the rise and use by terrorist groups of the internet. We are concerned about the self-radicalised actors who could strike with little or no notice."

CHAPTER 11
Confronting the Economic Issues of Islamic Society

"Long time men lay oppress'd with slavish fear;
Religion's tyranny did domineer ...
At length a mighty one of Greece began
T'assert the natural liberty of man,
By senseless terrors and vain fancies led
To slavery straight the conquer'd phantoms fled."

Lucretius, *De rerum Natura*, Bk. 1, 1. 63.

So far we have described the Islamic threat as we find it today and the response of the authorities and media to that situation. We must now address the more difficult and sensitive task of, a) Ascertaining measures that may be taken in countering the threat to world civilisation, and to the extent they may be justified; and, b) as to how the Islamic world may be reformed internally in dissipating both present and future conflict.

Before embarking on such a task, and to give some notion of authority for undertaking it, it may be apt to describe my personal connections with Islamic people over a period of several decades. During a life in international trade and throughout the 1980s, I spent much time in the Middle East, particularly in the Gulf States and Saudi Arabia, promoting the sale of British made products. Since that time Saudi Arabia, as the beating heart of the Islamic world, has both progressed and regressed. It has progressed in the obvious sense of building ever-more modern cities to accommodate its rapidly growing population, and it has regressed in the sense of becoming ever-more oppressive in introducing rules and regulations in emphasising its Wahabi culture, e.g., with regard to how Westerners should dress and banning the sale of Christmas cards.

Throughout history international traders have always been in the forefront as the renowned peacemakers of the world in promoting understanding amongst peoples and arranging the mutually beneficial exchange of goods. Unless the trader can empathise with foreigners in key positions and win their trust he cannot hope for commercial success. In the contemporary world this particularly applies to those seeking to trade with such a country as Saudi Arabia that is closed to the ordinary traveller. To enter the country one needs to be invited by a sponsor, at which point one may apply for a visa.

Saudis and most other Arabs only engage in trade with an individual, and have little concern or understanding for such an abstract concept as the company or corporation. Hence socialising for a period of several days is an essential prerequisite before any business negotiations are entered into. This entails drinking endless glasses of sweet tea, or Arabic coffee, and observing a strict etiquette whilst the subject of conversation often circles around the principles of religion. The atmosphere is relaxed and good-humoured, but there are subjects of discussion that are clearly off-limits, such as referring to or asking after female relatives.

As a guest one must naturally remain circumspect on questions of religion and be complimentary on all references to the Koran. On being invited into the family home for an evening meal, the extended male family of 15 to 20 persons may usually be present. The hospitality is gracious and indulgent, as the younger members pull out choice pieces of meat from the sheep's roasted carcase lying on a huge silver platter, to offer the foreign guests. Discreet proselytising gestures are occasionally made, and one is reminded that no good Muslim fails to "love Jesus," and that the Virgin Mary was the greatest woman who ever lived as she was "untouched by man." Although the foreigner may cherish the consolation of belonging to an Abrahamic faith of the "Book," and this carries some weight with his Muslim brother, he nonetheless remains an "infidel." The greatest compliment one may hope for is to be cheerfully told that one would "make a good Muslim."

After four or five days of such socialising, and aspiring to be the perfect courtier, thirty minutes may be spent in negotiating a business deal and an order may be written out on the back of an envelope which hopefully amounts to a huge quantity of goods. Whilst personal relationships are always cordial they are not necessarily transparent on either side. The foreigner cannot be entirely "accepted" or "belong" unless he converts to the Islamic faith. Over the past 100 years many Westerners have indeed converted to Islam, including noted travellers or those who have opted to work for the media or TV and settle for life in Saudi Arabia.

During the 90s and well into the present century my wife and I have lodged Muslim student guests from the Gulf States and Saudi Arabia for 6-monthly or yearly periods, and they have always been courteous and pleased to dine at our table – even tolerating the presence of a woman. Their stay in the West, however, has never seemed to alter their habits or ways of thinking. We have been awoken in the early hours by their movements on the call to prayer, and we have been conscientious with regard to their diet. In return they have been generous with gifts, and when socialising outside the house have always sought to mix with Muslims alone. None of our visitors ever sought the company of the opposite sex – and would have been horrified at the idea – so far as we could perceive.

On one occasion this gave rise to an event we found amusing. A young French lady (who knew nothing of Islamic life) at one time occupied a room adjoining with that of an Arab guest, and when several of the latter's friends gathered in his room to watch a Cup Final, our French guest who had no TV but was keen to follow the match, knocked on her neighbour's door and entered. Without further ado, she sat on one of the beds in front of the TV, and was astonished when the four or five Arabs who were also seated there, jumped up in horror and stood at the back of the room as far away as they could from the girl. The French lady, fully aware she had caused offence, left the room immediately, and afterwards complained to my wife and me, that they treated her as if she had the "plague," and could not understand their unfriendliness.

The above survey of personal relationships with the Islamic community is a necessary introduction to the attempt at objectivity in addressing the difficult task below. The closer one's personal relationship with an object for study, the more sympathetic one is assumed to be. In usual circumstances this would seem to create an additional difficulty. In standing by what is analysed as the ultimate or core truth of a matter, it is therefore necessary to expunge all those personal preferences, and all those pleasantries of personal contact that divert the mind from a higher truth or understanding. And that higher truth is the need to save world civilisation from the threat of annihilation. And the only weapon that is available to humankind for such a purpose is *Reason.*

As noted early in this book, the spirit and power for maintaining and promoting world civilisation is held in stewardship by the peoples of the northern hemisphere in conjunction with the Confucian peoples of the Far East, and the dominions of the Pacific. This is not to suggest that these countries are in political agreement on all matters. But they are in agreement on the need for modernity, and that the latter is dependent on Knowledge and free thought, and that religious fundamentalism is a poison which if uncontrolled may lead to terrorism, and possibly, even to the destruction of world civilisation.

There are many other non-Islamic countries that whilst in sympathy with those promoting civilisation lack the strength or clarity of thinking in advancing the cause. And then there are other countries in a more southern hemisphere with minority or majority Muslim populations that may either be moderate or extreme in their religiosity. These differences and degrees of problems amongst various peoples need to be openly recognised if the cause of world civilisation is to be properly focused.

As noted in an earlier chapter, the root cause of most conflicts are found in economic conditions, and this certainly pertains to the question of Islamic terrorism or extreme religiosity, and that cause is over-population. The only response to such a situation, howsoever blunt or in-compassionate it may sound, is that each nation state should be responsible for controlling its own population or accept the consequences thereof. It must also fall to each nation state to prevent the migration of excess populations to seek an alternative soil elsewhere as otherwise an undeclared invasion situation exists through default. The search for land has been the cause of war since pre-historical times, and as the potential for war in our own time is more terrible than it has ever been, there is now a greater reason for population control in those regions where over-population is found, and only the nation state is capable of organising the prevention of such conflict.

This leads immediately into the question of mass migrations into Europe from the Middle East, Africa, and further afield. The recent open door policy of Angela Merkel in Germany was clearly philanthropic in intention and should be applauded for that reason, but did it best contribute to advancing world civilisation in contrast to other contrary factors? The answer has to be in the negative for a number of reasons: Firstly, if philanthropic motives are upheld against the need for upholding the survival of civilisation and the future of humanity, the first must surrender to the latter. The ethical reason for this is to ensure maximising the diminution of suffering that is attained through all the benefits of preserving and promoting World civilisation as against risks to the latter through the consequences of uncontrolled migration. It is a question of upholding the longer as contrasted with the shorter term. This does not remove the responsibility of the civilised world from relieving the suffering of the oppressed, but only that alternative means should be found for relieving it.

Secondly, such a policy introduces a high birth rate people into a low birth rate population that over time will inevitably undermine the cultural integrity of the nation states affected. Thirdly, it entails the introduction of an un-assimilable people on account of their intense religiosity. Fourthly, although educable in a conventional sense, such people are averse to freedom of thought. Fifthly, although demanding for personal rights, on the other hand, they are unprepared to take on the obligations of democratic responsibility; and Sixthly, they are generally employed in low-level occupations, whilst those with initiative tend to drift into the criminality of drug dealing or petty theft.

Mass migration should be clearly differentiated from the migration of the independent individual from one country to another for any reason whatsoever. Whilst the first amounts to an invasion, the second is no more than an excursion. The mass migrant may not arrive on the shores of Europe armed with a rifle or hand grenade, but he is nonetheless an invader as if he had arrived in a tank with all guns blazing. His final purpose is the same, i.e., to occupy a new land and grab its resources for his own benefit. This predominantly takes the form of housing and food. This does not mean that the European is turfed out of his home at bayonet point, or that he is reduced to starvation, but it does mean that house prices are raised in response to property shortages – and migrants are always privileged over ordinary citizens with the immediate grant of dwellings – and it does mean that food prices are increased. These are the inescapable facts arising from the pressures of over-population.

As for the millions from the southern hemisphere pushing towards Europe, counter-measures need to be taken now. Until the recent past most foreigners in any Continental country needed to register with the police. During my ten years in Germany and Scandinavia in the 1960s I registered annually with the police, or on every change of address, and my landlords were likewise obliged to register their foreign residents. In this way the police were able to keep tracks on aliens, and call them in for questioning at any time, usually with regard to the renewal of work permits. Any contravention of the rules might lead to deportation at any time. Much has happened since then. In Britain the police have rarely been involved with the supervision of foreigners, and now the chickens have come home to roost with an estimated million plus illegal immigrants. In Germany, meanwhile, the police are hardly involved with the new migrant situation.

As a minimum condition for entry into Europe, I would tentatively suggest that all migrants be registered from day 1, and charged a fee sufficient to cover administration costs. Those unable to pay such costs should be sent to Accommodation Centres where they are employed to cover board, lodging, and administration fees. In reducing the occurrence of poverty, vagrancy, and crime, I would suggest that national parliaments debate and legislate on the following:- 1. That Alien Havens be established on a departmental, county, or provincial basis, to which migrants may be held until further decisions are made, the costs to be borne by local or provincial authorities; and, 2. That Transit Camps be established pending early deportation to a Muslim territory or some other Third world nation state. In the first instance attempts should be made to return migrants to their countries of origin.

A far more difficult question arises with regard to those Islamic people long settled in Europe, most of whom already possess the passports of their host country. How are they to be regarded in view of their voluntary segregation, their contempt for Western values, and their retention of Islamic modes and dress? The official view is that we live in a tolerant multi-cultural society, but there exists a total incompatibility between Muslim and non-Muslim peoples arising from the religious totalitarianism of the former.

The cultural problem of Muslims arising from their excess religiosity has not only occurred in Western Europe in recent times. It occurred in the Balkans in the 1990s, and more significantly in India during the transition Independence period in 1947 when several million Muslims and Hindus were slaughtered during the mob-rule transfer of populations in the creation of Pakistan. Such bloodshed could never have happened if it was not for an underlying hatred motivated by cultural incompatibility between different peoples.

The theory of British, and indeed, of modern European society, is that there must be equal rights for all, but this is hardly a happy practicality when Muslims claim so many privileges stemming from the differences of Sharia law. English women, for example, are unlikely to be satisfied by the simple divorce proceedings and totally unfair decisions of the Sharia courts. It is not only absurd but chaotic to have more than one legal system in a country, although in pre-Revolutionary France there were many such systems, and that led to acts of gross injustice that had eventually to be overthrown.

If Muslims choose and act in such a way as to culturally and legally separate themselves from their host society, and at the same time insist on grabbing all the benefits of that society, they cannot rightfully have their cake and eat it. This does not mean they should be made into "second class citizens," for such a term is meaningless in itself, but their separateness should be given a legal definition so that a proper and clear basis should be given for the discussion of their wishes. In other words the *equality principle* should not be applied when we intend the *difference principle*, for if the former is referred to, the ridiculous situation will arise when the entire population is obliged to follow the will of Islamic society.

The "Ferdinand and Isabella" solution to the problem would be unthinkable to most, but in the past it has been suggested in Parliament that state funds might be used in returning those to their countries of origin or ancestry if they so desired. Such a policy if carried out by a single state would be quite impractical on economic grounds, but if the proposal was presented as a pan-European initiative, it could become a subject for debate. But better still, in avoiding such a course, is the hope of reforming the Islamic world internally in dissipating a conflict situation with those beyond the faith. And it is to that subject we must now turn.

It is my belief that a peaceful settlement may be reached between Islamic and non-Islamic peoples but only through a proper course of educational measures. From the start, the dangerous dogma of "multi-culturalism" as a universal panacea for peaceful relationships must be ditched forever. It is dangerous because of its deception and the hidden and unconscious forces lying in the hearts of most people. I describe these forces as *unconscious* rather than *suppressed* because the majority live out their lives in a spirit of benevolence towards all with whom they come into contact, irrespective of race, nationality, or language, etc. To live in a state of mental enmity is intolerable to most. Hence peace in civil society is the natural state of existence.

But throughout history there have been innumerable examples of mixed societies, usually of different language rather than racial groups, which whilst they remain in concord for the greater period of time, break out endemically into conflict resulting in terrible bloodshed. To those at a distance, such horrors are witnessed with astonishment and appear inexplicable. Why should different peoples appear harmonious on one day, and the next be at each other's throats? The explanation, of course, is usually complex and economic. But every such conflict has a moral tale to tell.

As with every animal species Homo Sapiens need to live in distinctively defined groups. In advanced societies this takes the form of the Nation State – the most precious entity, after the family, to which any human can belong. This fact is now recognised by British leaders of both the left and right, and over recent years there has been much talk about the need for "promoting Britishness." Our leading statesman may have a hazy notion of what Nationality is, but they are struggling to understand the concept after a long period when the political environment has tended to eschew national ideals in favour of a very messy and undefined internationalism.

In setting the idea of Nationality within a modern framework, it needs to be understood that each nation state has a distinctive identity that needs to be respected by every other. Language, customs, religion, and natural boundaries generally define the nation state, and each needs to safeguard its cultural and economic integrity. In another book I have demonstrated clearly that democracy as an overall form of government is only workable long-term in the nation state.[16] Nations may vary greatly in their character according to traditions, geographical circumstances, etc., but even amongst closely similar and contiguous countries, such as those of Scandinavia or the Benelux group, there are sharp differences and pretensions of

---

[16] See my book, *The Democratic Imperative: the reality of power relationships in the Nation State.*

dislike – although when faced by a serious external threat, I have no doubt they would band together in defending underlying values.

A culture defines a nation state, and cultures are traceable to the source of a civilisation to which they belong. Just as a civilisation may be major or minor, or in growth or decline, or in a state of recovery or resurgence, as in the Far East, so the same principles may be applied to the culture of the nation state. The civilisation of the West, which inherits its values from the Romano-Hellenic and Judaeo civilisations of the ancient world, is the most significant in the world today on account of its technological advance, but in the very near future it is likely to link up as an equal with the Confucian civilisations of the Far East, in deciding on the destiny of the future.

Progressive civilisations and cultures need to be dynamic or in a constant state of change. That is, they cannot merely sit on a huge heritage of learning and wisdom and claim superiority over the rest of the world based on past events. Such civilisations or nations thereby condemn themselves to precipitous decline, as occurred with Byzantium in the middle ages, or China and Japan in the 16th and 17th centuries onwards. Progressive civilisations need to exert political power through the never-ending advance of both theoretical ideas and technological development.

Higher cultures have a unique advantage over those that are inferior in that they are increasingly diverse and better able to absorb foreign influences without sacrificing their essential integrity. Lower cultures, by contrast, that are invariably bounded by all kinds of strict customs and rules of life, and a narrow understanding of reality are not merely undermined, but often quickly destroyed after contact or absorption by a higher culture.

Much has been written about alcohol in destroying primitive cultures, but that is a crude example of the process. There are a thousand other incidental ways in which primitive peoples have unknowingly been destroyed – even by those who sought to perpetuate their cultures. The romantic Rousseauen idea of the "noble savage," or that primitive peoples lead free and happy lives has long been exploded as a myth by the researches of anthropologists. The reality is that primitive peoples are so enslaved by taboos and superstitious custom that they have little opportunity for true freedom that springs from knowledge.

The evolution of humankind through the acquisition of knowledge is an ethical as well as a technological process, for the assessment of ethical values can only be properly understood in the light of comprehending the mind and the underlying psychological needs for a truly fulfilling existence. It is these facts that justify the cause of world civilisation as defined at the beginning of this book. And it is why all measures must be taken to counteract threats to the survival of that civilisation.

CHAPTER 12
Secular versus Divine Ethics

"I fear the iron yoke of outward conformity hath left a slavish
print upon our necks."

John Milton, *Prose Works*, Vol II, p. 97.

The observant reader will at this point be startled by the
relevance of the concluding paragraphs of the previous
chapter to the central theme of this book. Islamic Wahabi
civilisation feels itself to be very vulnerable in the modern
world, and that is the reason for its aggression. For three
centuries it has been safely insulated by the expanses and heat of
impenetrable desert from contamination by "infidel foreigners,"
and it was only the consequences of the wealth-generating
internal combustion engine that allowed it to stomp around the
world stage. No country in the world has so securely
safeguarded its frontiers as Saudi Arabia for ideological
purposes – not even the Soviet Union.

None of this is to suggest that the Islamic Wahabi culture
is inferior in the ordinary sense, or when aligned against other
cultures is below the medium, or objectively may be categorised
as inferior. But it is lopsided, and it is a civilisation that stands
alone. The genius of Islamic culture is to be found in its poetry,
and especially in the Koran. Listening to the chanting of the
Koran is one of the greatest aesthetic experiences of the spoken
word. In Saudi Arabia there is a 24-hour radio channel enabling
the listener to hear the Koran at any time of the day or night, and
during my visits to the country, my sponsor always tuned into
this station when driving. The beauty of the language exerts a
most hypnotic effect, and clearly it is a powerful influence on all
believers tuning into the channel.

But the beauty of the Koran, as with the King James Bible,
or the reverberating chanting of Old Slavonic in a Russian
Orthodox church, is an aesthetic rather than a moral or ethical
experience, and although it may inspire virtuous thoughts and

good deeds, the excitation of its technique on the nervous system, may just as well inspire the use of the sword and the shedding of blood. Such age-old religious texts were designed to arouse the passions, but they were unable to ensure that such passions were directed towards benign or malign purposes. The song of the spoken word is often more powerful than its intended message. For this reason, therefore, the King James Bible is often in safer hands in those of a declared atheist like Richard Dawkins, who has spoken eloquently on the aesthetic and literary value of the book, than in the hands of many a priest with a dodgy grasp of morality.

In passing a serious judgement on the same book, it is my opinion that the Old Testament presents the world's greatest study of resentment, whilst the New Testament best expresses the need for compassion in all instances of suffering. All ancient religious texts should be examined from the viewpoint of psychological interpretation if they are to be made relevant for the modern world. When it comes to morality, or ethical issues, then these are matters for the study and decision of the purely secular mind, the outcome of which may then be passed back to religious leaders of different faiths for propagating amongst their congregations. This should be the future of religion if it is to maintain seriousness in itself, and more significantly, retain the conviction of the majority.

The contemporary problem of Islam, therefore, is quite unique. It is a lopsided culture because of its extreme religiosity and because it lacks a secular dimension. It is cut off entirely from an intellectual understanding of the modern world, and cannot even begin to grasp the foundations of modern ethical thinking. This is a terrible situation for a culture based entirely on religion for ethics is the starting point for any serious approach to religious thought. Whilst the Muslim applauds the penalty of stoning to death for apostasy, and thousands will press forward in gleeful vengeance in witnessing such executions in the public squares of their cities, such scenes are horrific to Westerners and other non-Muslims because we believe in free thought and free choice, and that anyone has a right to believe or disbelieve in anything providing no harm is brought to another.

But the Muslim, as with all religious enthusiasts, is only prepared to believe in what is found in religious texts, or the Hadith, or accepted customs passed down from umpteen generations. He is not prepared to use his free reason, or attempt at objectivity, because that would be *profanity*. The Muslim does not use the word *secular* because that gives a positive gloss to free thought, but he constantly reverts to the word *profane* for that is a pejorative term expressing all his contempt for non-religious thought. If he were confronted with the idea that it is unjust to kill a man because he repudiates his faith, he would quickly reply that his death was necessary in preventing others from following his example.

The problem of resolving the incompatibility between the Islamic and non-Islamic modes of thought is therefore immense. Such a backward culture should never have achieved the power that it has in the modern world to present such a terrorist threat, and I cannot recollect any comparable situation in world history of the entanglement of two such contrasting and incompatible civilisations. The cause of this situation is only accountable to the need to fill our petrol tanks; the age-old negotiating skills of Arabs in pressing a hard bargain; and the mountains of gold they have received for the minerals beneath their sands.

Three approaches may be made in attempting to resolve the situation: a) The formulation of a secular Enlightenment addressed to the Islamic world; b) The internal reform of Islam from within in meeting the demands of the modern world; and, c) The cultural integration of Muslims into the different nation states in which they happen to be situated. The above touch on overlapping areas, but whilst b) should be left to the leading initiative of the Muslim population, a) and c) require the input and active encouragement of the non-Muslim world.

Modern civilisation since the start of the 16th century, and aggressively so since the start of the 18th, has been essentially secular, without which free thought, science, and technological advance would have been impossible. Religiosity has blocked the Muslim's road to self-improvement, or genuine independence, or what in the West is described as "a place in the sun." All his discontents and resentments that have led to worldwide terror are not due to his "oppression" by others, but rather by his mental incapacity to advance his personal progress. Whilst on the one hand he has been showered with wealth, that has proved a superficial rather than a *real* benefit to his future, on the other hand he has languished in ignorance and supine leisure as foreigners have been called upon to undertake anything of a technical nature, irrespective of whether it be in the oil industry or medicine, or town planning, or architecture, etc.

He may not even be aware that his discontents are of his own making, but instead regard the wealth with which he is showered is merely intended to pay for his advanced material needs, so he may meanwhile pray and thank God for the gifts so bestowed. Such a misuse of resources is not merely foolish, but a form of self-imposed infantilism, a Peter Pan syndrome, a child reluctant or unable to take on responsibility for that which he facilitated through contractual arrangements in the first place. In this context religion becomes a form of enslavement, enabling a satisfying complacency with a good conscience. Confronting secularism may amount to a course in shock therapy, but to the enquiring or intelligent mind, it should reveal the light of huge vistas of new knowledge, and as the cobwebs and phantoms of past illusions fall apart, the inspiration of new realities take their form.

None of this is possible without the motivation of curiosity, and the calm intelligence of the open mind, but these things are anathema to religious authority that so often demands unquestioning obedience to the downright absurd – or even the wicked – as well as to the commonsensical. Until the Muslim has the courage to cross the dividing line between the religious and the secular he has no chance of achieving Enlightenment. In the face of such difficulty, his best opportunity is to take the ethical path in examining what really constitutes good and evil, but even then he will need to study the psychology of the human mind, and weigh such issues as freewill and determinism, and how these impact on personal responsibility, differing degrees of guilt, and the roles of compassion and punishment.

As soon as he has resolved the question of ethics from a secular standpoint, he will then be better empowered to examine broader social, scientific and philosophical problems from a realistic or incontrovertible perspective, and as he progresses, his confidence and understanding of the world will increase with ever greater clarity. In this and through the strength of reason he will discover his truer self, his liberation from the shackles of the past, and a guiding light for the future. His commitment to secularism does not mean he need forego religion, but his commitment to religion may then be transferred to a rational basis, freed from the doctrine of revelation, but founded on a social bonding mechanism embracing the highest spiritual ethical ideals.

In addressing an enlightening aspect of Islamic religion, viz., in defining the nature of God, the Western intellectual tradition may be in an exceptionally advantageous position. There were a number of 18th century thinkers who went hot and cold in their evaluation of Islam, but what is most significant is that the religion, as an object of comparison, was sometimes used as a weapon to attack the Catholic church in France, or in England, to cast a disdainful shadow on religion generally. The simple and unpretentious concept of the One God was attractive to our discerning ancestors, and they compared this favourably with the absurd gymnastics and jumping through hoops of the Trinity or the man-God who was allowed to be crucified by his own father. Voltaire led the pack in his voluminous writings on the abuses and tyranny of the church, and the contradictions of its sacred book. In adopting a self-effacing stance, these are writings that perhaps may be used in discussion in cultivating a closer religious affinity with our Muslim brothers and sisters, in coming nearer to their conception of God. It would entail a mutual exchange of rational sentiments on an important matter, and it is rationality that is most desired in bringing the two civilisations together.

We must begin by ascertaining the present intellectual situation of the Salafi movement within Saudi Arabia in its attempt at reform or modernism. Salafism is an ultra-conservative fundamentalist reform movement within Sunnah or Hadith Islam. If this sounds contradictory, it is. It has often been described as a hybrid of Wahabism and post-1960s movements. Some have, rightly or wrongly, regarded Salafism as identical with Wahabism, but the former regard such a definition as "derogatory." Salafists are divided into three categories: firstly, the *Purists* or "quietists," the largest group who avoid politics; secondly, the *Activists*, the second largest group, who become involved in politics; and thirdly, the *Jihadists*, who are most radical and not prepared to eschew terrorist tactics.

As for many years dozens of thinkers, both within Saudi Arabia and beyond, have been actively engaged in dispute on questions of reform and modernism, this might give the impression to the Westerner of a great enlightened debate holding out a promise for the future. It should be borne in mind, however, that such intellectual activity is pursued within the bubble of Koranic and Islamic teaching. As doctrines and dogmas must not be overstepped, the slightest suspicion of heretical tendencies are jumped upon by other reformers as unacceptable, and this leads inevitably to vicious internecine conflicts. It would be naïve to suppose that such prospective reformers were united by a well-intentioned feeling of mutual support.

If their internal divisions were not sufficient to block their progress, the eagle eye of the state would attend to blocking any further hope for success. Many political prisoners are held at any one time, some for short periods, others for many years, and some who are arrested and released on a frequent basis. Whilst the religious authorities are seemingly ruthless in prosecuting intellectuals on the flimsiest pretexts, it is only fair to remark that there are others who are arrested on grounds that would justify the same in England, the Netherlands, or any other West European country. Such charges are not based on "the right to free speech," but rather for inciting public disorder or such outrages as the violent expulsion of the Royal family.

Such reformers and modernists too often lack the common sense need for discretion, or the careful use of irony or satire, or the gentle humour or elegance of expression of our 18th century French or English thinkers designed to deflect the anger of their intended victims. Again we are confronted by the black and white mould of the Semitic mind with its tendency to extremism, and lack of subtlety.

But there is a more significant impediment: if the imprisonment of religious-political dissidents in Saudi Arabia is hardly mentioned in the Western press, it is not because there is a lack of interest in human rights, but because the charges for their alleged crimes or misdemeanours are incomprehensible to the Westerner. That is, because untranslatable Arabic religious terms would need to be used in explaining what those offences actually were. At every step we return to the question of *Divine politics*, and in the secular non-Islamic world, we cannot recognise that any such thing exists in reality. This seems to create an impossible barrier for dialogue between the two opposing sides.

In view of this problem, it might be thought helpful to turn to an established Arabic scholar, who has studied these questions and has written extensively on them for a number of years. Madawi Al-Rasheed is in fact a Saudi citizen, a political exile working in Britain, whose return to her own country would risk arrest and incarceration. Her numerous books and papers are banned in her own country, but her latest work, *Muted Modernists: The Struggle over Divine Politics in Saudi Arabia*, attempts to end on an optimistic note when she writes, "I hope this book has shown that reform within an Islamic framework can be a viable, albeit difficult, agenda in a country that is yet to experience full mobilisation in the pursuit of equitable and representative government."[17] My final impression, on the other hand, is that these closing words are little more than diplomatic courtesy used as a cover for an underlying pessimism she is

---

[17] *Muted Modernists*, Hurst & Co., 2015, p. 163.

reluctant to openly admit. My careful reading of her scholarly and closely researched book can lead, unfortunately, to no other conclusion.

It would be apt to list the names of several leading Saudi thinkers who, nonetheless, are striving to resolve the difficult questions confronting their country and the wider world, and where they stand in the present debate. All the following have been described as trained in religious studies without necessarily having become religious scholars. There is Salman al-Awdah, who preaches in study circles about Ramadan rituals, and moves out of his role as a preacher and becomes a political dissident the moment he tweets a statement denouncing repression and the unlawful detention of human rights activists. And then there is Abdullah al-Maliki, who represents a new generation of Islamist intellectuals who draw their sources from outside the Islamic tradition to express the importance of choice rather than compulsion in religious observance. He was reported as being enchanted by the Arab uprisings of 2011.

Muhammad Al-abd-al-Karim, on the other hand, was prepared to stretch the limits of interpretation to deconstruct the religious roots of oppression, injustice and absolute rule. He sees Islam as a form of monotheistic awakening and an opportunity to free people from servitude and oppression. And lastly, we may consider Muhammid al-Almari,who goes beyond Salafi reservations on democracy to advocate it as the only solution. His book on democracy represents one of the strongest Saudi endorsements of a political system that has long been rejected by mainstream Salafis.

The above gives the impression of a political environment that is very opaque or nebulous. It is never quite certain what is really meant in practical terms. For a "proper" definition of terms it is necessary to turn to Koranic or closely associated sources, but as these are open to differing interpretations, again this leads to confusion. There are infinite opportunities for misunderstanding and petty quarrels, and sometimes violent acts are committed through the use of words by others that were never intended in such a direction. The source of blame is almost invariably traceable to sacred and incontrovertible texts that have never been questioned, but nonetheless, have been quoted and used in a wide variety of situations over the centuries. The authority is always that of God, whose commands are infallible, and in whom we may ever trust. He needs no Reason for his authority for that is the wretched support of lowly man alone.

In such a political environment, where can the Muslim turn in seeking true enlightenment in the wider world? In such a situation one is forced to resurrect the old Irish joke about the lost traveller asking for directions. The answer given is that, "If I were you, I wouldn't start from here." In other words, the Muslim must throw over completely his religious mindset in taking up an entirely secular stance in the consideration of social or political issues. He can do no other. He needs to break from the imprisoning framework that prevents his free use of reason in the light of the material modern world. His spirituality based on ancient textual obedience is a false spirituality of lies and delusion. As long as he follows such a course in attempting to resolve the woes of the world, he is no more than a dog running around in circles chasing its own tail.

CHAPTER 13
The Path to Islamic Enlightenment

"Religion does not censure or exclude
Unnumber'd pleasures, harmlessly pursu'd."

William Cowper, *Retirement*, 1. 783.

Islam needs an Enlightenment in meeting the reality of the contemporary world, and in the first instance, it needs its own Voltaire with the wit and humour to explode all the myths and falsehood of discredited beliefs. Who may be sought who has the courage, the conviction and imaginative breadth to raise such a flag? It should preferably come from someone close to the highest political authority – someone with the strength and credibility to challenge the Wahabi leadership – someone prepared to place his head above the parapet. It might be suggested that no such individuals exist, but I would doubt such a contention.

The world is full of variety, even when it seems most homogeneous. When in Qatar, a quarter of a century ago, I worked in partnership with one of the wealthiest families in the country, and lodged in their hotel on the outskirts of Doha. The son of my sponsor was a student of psychiatry, and the latter's professor was sent out from England to spend time with his student. Every afternoon the two would relax around the poolside for four or five hours, deep in conversation on philosophy and social issues, as the younger man absorbed the wisdom and knowledge of the elder. I have no doubt that there were (and still are) hundreds of similar young men and women in the Middle East who are hungry to understand the civilisation of the West. The problem is, that in view of their usual isolation, and the nature of the religiously totalitarian societies in which they exist, their impact on their peers is likely to be negligible.

There is also another fear amongst the ruling authorities of Islamic states: if Muslims surrender to accepting the ideas, customs, and beliefs of the non-Islamic world, will they not risk losing their Islamic identity? What will be left of the Muslim if he surrenders to the Westernising process? If secularism is incompatible with Islam, what then? This conundrum explains the aggressiveness of the Muslim worldwide. If he does not seek to conquer – to condemn the infidel – he will eventually be subjugated by forces beyond his strength. He cannot conceive in his own heart that the Islamic and non-Islamic worlds can genuinely coexist in peace and harmony.

There is, therefore, only one solution to the problem, viz., the creation of a secular Islam for secular Muslims, so that the latter may retain his identity with confidence and pride, whilst meanwhile adapting his approach to religious issues. How is this possible? There is already a precedent for such a transformation. If the Arab peoples are prepared to glance at the history of their fellow Semites, the Jews, they may indeed uncover an inspiring example.

Up until the 18th century Jewish communities in Europe were no less self-enclosed and isolated from gentile life than are Islamic peoples today. The Jews had their own ghettoes, their own customs, laws, and their own way of dress, which segregated them with disdain from the general population to no lesser degree than their unpopularity for lending at interest or alleged sharp practice in business. It may be argued that the Jews were more unpopular throughout the medieval and early modern period than are Islamic peoples at the present point in time.

But in the wake of the European Enlightenment, a group of Jews in central and eastern Europe founded their own enlightenment or *Haskalah*, which was centred in Berlin, already renowned as a secular, multi-cultural and multi-ethnic centre, offering a fertile environment for radical movements. The proponents of the *Haskalah* were known as the *Maskilim*, and amongst their leading thinkers was the Prussian, Moses Mendelssohn (1729-86), the Pole, Isaac Satanov (1735-1805), Naphtali Hirz Wessely (1725-1805) from Hamburg, Aaron Halle-Wolfssohn (1754-1835), and Joseph Perl (1773-1839).

The movement flourished between the 1770s and the 1880s, and their main intention was to encourage integration within the various nation states of Jewish communities. Although they clashed initially with the conservative and rabbinical elite, and criticised such traits of Jewish society as child marriage, the commonsense of their secularism, soon won around the support of the educated majority to their calls for reform. They called upon their followers to leave the ghetto both physically and mentally; to reject traditional in favour of modern dress; to uphold the national spirit or their nation state; and in learned circles, to promote an increase in the use of Hebrew and less in the use of Yiddish.

The success of the *Haskalah* was followed in the mid-19th century with the emergence of Reform Judaism – sometimes described as Liberal or Progressive Judaism. Again, this was a German-inspired movement, formulated by the eminent academic scholar, Rabbi Abraham Geiger (1810-74), and a group of associates. It was a major confessional division within Judaism, emphasising the evolving nature of the religion, and the priority of its ethical values over its ceremonial aspects, and a belief in a continuous revelation not centred on the theophany at Mount Sinai. It held Judaic law as basically non-binding, and advocated greater openness to external influences and progressive values.

Abraham Geiger began his programme of religious reform through adapting the synagogue liturgy. For example, he abolished the prayers of mourning for the Temple, believing that since Jews were German citizens, such prayers might appear to be disloyal to the ruling powers and could ignite anti-Semitism. His studies at the universities of Heidelberg and Bonn had given him a good insight to the secular society of Germany, but perhaps of most interest was his doctoral thesis awarded through the University of Marburg, following an in-depth study of the Koran, entitled, *What did Muhammid take from Judaism?* His conclusions are that Mohammed took a great deal from Judaism, particularly with regard to understanding the monotheistic nature of God.

At the present day Reform Judaism embodies two denominations: the American Union of Reform Judaism, and the British Movement for Reform Judaism. Along with other regional branches sharing the same convictions, such as British Liberal Judaism, they are members of the World for Progressive Judaism, established in 1926, and Reconstructionist Judaism, espousing an unrelated doctrine, entered the Union in 1990. The outcome of the *Haskalah* and Reform Judaism has not only culminated in the complete enfranchisement of the Jewish people worldwide, but more significantly, has enabled them to achieve leading positions in the arts and sciences and other major professions and occupations, in the leading industrial economies.

It should also be noted that great numbers of Jews are non-religious, or even atheistic, but nonetheless retain a pride in their Judaism. The Jewish identity is strictly based on race, i.e., one cannot convert to Judaism except through extraordinary circumstances and a protracted process. It is therefore all the more remarkable they have integrated so successfully into the societies of the major countries of the world. Their racial identity certainly overrides their religion. Judaism is possibly the only religion in the world that is non-proselytising, and in this important sense it has not offered a threat to others. As a North Londoner who has had close and friendly contacts with Jews since my early schooldays, I have on a number of occasions encountered Jews who have snorted with contempt at any mention of their ultra-Orthodox brethren whom they labelled as "fanatics." The secular Jew may have as great a variety of opinions as any gentile.

In view of the above, is it therefore inconceivable that the Muslim cannot retain his true Islamic identity through adopting a secular lifestyle? All it needs is a leap of the imagination, an honest attitude to truth, and a taste for freedom – and most of all the will to oppose the tyranny of religious totalitarianism. Although Islam is more indebted to Judaism than any other religious tradition, and although they share similar Semitic languages, they have otherwise developed in different directions. There is no possibility for the self-improvement or modernisation of Islamic peoples except through a radical enlightenment as experienced by their Jewish brothers and sisters. But are they prepared to undergo such an experience? It may be that their religion in combination with the high living standards enjoyed by Gulf Arabs have generated a lethargy and complacency that makes the prospects for any kind of change unattractive.

Although the total number of Gulf Arabs may represent a small fraction of all Muslims in the world it should be borne in mind that they are by far the dominating influence through the Wahabism of the peninsula; the huge financial proselytising power of the Saudi state; and the fact that Mecca and Medina, those centres of pilgrimage for the Haj, draw the Muslims of the world for at least a one-time life experience. Whilst a century ago, in far-flung places, Islam may have developed many liberal attitudes and practices that would shock the contemporary Arab, the influence of the latter is now being enforced through both the propaganda of legally established authorities and the terror of all-powerful rebel groups.

Whilst it may be true that a mental lethargy is most responsible for hindering the growth of new ideas, it is equally true that the overhanging threat of an ultra-conservative establishment bringing unspecified condign punishment in its wake holds the majority in a permanent state of fear. I believe that this is the only explanation for the disgraceful response of silence by Muslims in the face of terrorist outrages. No Muslim has as yet effectively made his voice heard in the face of the breakdown of law and order, and for this state of denial, all must share the shame and blame for what has occurred. The voice of protest needs to be heard loud and clear. But how is it to be realised?

As it is necessary that such protest immediately engages the mind of the educated Muslim, it must begin with a philosophical critique of Islamic theology, perhaps through popularising the ideas of Spinoza's *Tractatus Theologico-Politicus* (1670) and re-publishing the leading articles of

Bayle's *Dictionaire historique et critique* (1697) touching on religious issues. Attention could then be turned to the rationalism of Descartes, and the empirical philosophy of Hobbes, Locke and Hume. By the time the Muslim has absorbed the writings of the latter, he should have a complete understanding of the value of reason in serving the better interests of humankind – as well as the meaning of truth.

A close study of the history of the West over the past five centuries would also be invaluable, in grasping the evils of religiosity, and the benefits and happiness emerging from enlightened views. The prime example of a foreign country that always maintained its independence and cultural integrity, and yet was totally transformed into a modern state through studying the history of the West, was Japan. The success of Japan, and the worldwide respect she now commands, could act as a leading inspiration for the Islamic peoples.

As soon as a secular Islam has been created, the reform of religion may be attended to. It is not suggested that secularists should forego their religion, but that the latter should be relegated to a private role in life. Perhaps prayers could be reduced from five to two times daily, on rising and retiring and be performed with privacy at the bedside as with the majority of people, and that services (or public prayers) in the mosque should only be held on Friday. Whilst images or pictorial representation may continue to be forbidden in religious places, and burial remain anonymous as it is today, moves should be taken to repudiate the anti-life Puritanism of Wahabi beliefs as manifested in so many spheres of Islamic life.

The greatest evil at the present time is the segregation of the sexes, for the consequences of this creates an intolerable psychological burden for both men and women. It is probable that the pressures of segregation are the sole cause – tipping the balance – in enabling the terrorism and suicide bombing we witness today. How else can the universal death wish be explained? To die in joy for Allah is no more than a perversion arising from sexual repression. The extreme aggression of Islamic men is only accountable to the fact they are denied the company of women and hence the need to seek another outlet for their hormonal testosterone. It is equally abnormal, or contrary to human nature, that young women should seek to destroy themselves as living bombs, or flee to Syria in the hope of marrying a man who will be martyred in the cause of Islam. This *Liebestod* is only made possible through the accumulation of sexual tension that can never be satisfied in the real world.

No other major society in the world today imposes such repression on its young people, and if we may contradict this statement by citing Spain, in the recent past, or Sicily or India, at the present time, it is only because these territories remained for centuries under Islamic rule. If Islamic peoples are to be freed from the burdens of the past, then the first step is to liberate their womenfolk. Until 30 or so years ago Arabian women were confined to the home, and their only leisure pursuits were dancing or singing amongst themselves or reading the Koran. They are still confined to the home, but since that time, their educational opportunities have been greatly extended. A university education has infinitely widened their horizons although their career options still remain within a narrow margin.

It is my impression through contact at trade fairs in the Kingdom, or on those rare occasions in a public place when a man has actually introduced me to his wife, that Saudi women are probably better educated than the men – certainly in regard to their foreign language abilities. Such educational standards are not of course accountable to career opportunities, but rather to loving knowledge for its own sake – and because it is freely available – and not least, because it is the only alternative to the monotonous and soul-destroying pursuit of dancing and singing within four blank walls. I have found Saudi women to have a relaxed and cheerful manner, to talk about practical and common sense matters – and never to touch on religion.

In preventing an anarchic situation, or the breakdown of state authority, Islamic reform should be promoted by the leading families of each nation state in a series of gradual stages through a five-year plan. Hence the emancipation of women should begin at the apex of society with the gradual Westernising of dress through government edicts, culminating in the uncovering of hair. Inevitably, such changes will be met by shock and outrage in the early stages, as they were in early 18th century Russia at the behest of Peter the Great, but (as in Russia) this would be lessened by the call to follow the lead of the upper classes. As soon as such reforms had been fully achieved amongst the top layers of society, they may then be applied to the middle classes, and when they in their turn have completed the transformation, the lower classes may be authorised to follow in the steps of their betters. Only through such a mode of state-regulated authority could modernisation be achieved in preventing the risk of open rebellion under the leadership of religious reactionaries.

Only through the same methods, i.e., from the top downwards, could further reforms be initiated. The Westernisation of male dress would follow, culminating in the prohibition of beards and moustaches – and no exemption taxes should be allowed in the attempt to avoid such regulations. There would then be the need to repeal the Illegal Seclusion laws, and an officially written etiquette designed for enabling socialisation between men and women. Whilst child and arranged marriages and polygamy would be forbidden, as it already is in the Islamic country of Turkey, men and women would be free to choose their own partners.

Although so-called "free love" or promiscuity should be discouraged, to help ensure the success of marriage, engaged couples should be obliged by law to live together for three months prior to the wedding day. This would be to ensure that impotency, or other disfunctions, or adverse homosexual inclinations, etc., are uncovered in advance, so that a potentially unhappy marriage may be prevented in good time. As Sir Thomas More proposed a similar cautionary arrangement in his book *Utopia* more than 500 years ago I see no reason for irresolution on such a matter in the 21st century. In the Islamic world divorce is often made an easier option in a variety of circumstances than it is in the non-Islamic world, but in view of the seriousness of the institution of marriage, I believe it should only be entered into after ascertaining the certainties for its success.

Lastly, but perhaps of most significance, a more professional approach should be taken with regard to organising the reformation of the Islamic church on a hierarchical basis. Religious teachers should only be taken on for religious training after they have qualified to degree level in the secular subjects of Western philosophy, psychology, and post-Renaissance history. Having studied in depth the subject of ethics from a secular perspective, they would then be properly qualified to preach the teachings of the Koran and Hadith without the risk of creating mischief. A proper licensing system, and the watchful eye of a hierarchical priesthood committed to moderate religiosity and the demands of reason, would ensure a religious Islam committed to the demands of the modern world.

It may be enquired as to why more democratic methods are not proposed in seeking the reformation of Islamic society. Quite apart from the instinctive antipathy of the Muslim for democratic procedures, as being based on the promotion of populism as opposed to virtue – and this must be respected – history has clearly demonstrated that there are frequent situations when resort to democratic methods leads to destruction and bloodshed, rather than to reform and progress. Whilst democracy should be the end purpose of all societies, it is only achievable as a successful system through the slow evolutionary conflict of groups at the apex of society peacefully settling their differences, and then allowing the values of such a system to permeate downward to the rest of the community. Democracy cannot simply be imposed on a people unaccustomed to its features through the rule of law, nor should it be, as the attempt is doomed to failure.

The subject of this book has been to resolve the problem of Islam as we find it in the world today, and only extraordinary measures can hope to resolve an extraordinary situation. Hence no apology is made for the path we have attempted to tread. In any event, there are only two courses for the future: either Islam plucks up the courage to confront the religious elite and carry out its own internal reforms; or else, economic forces will eventually destroy it from within and bring down the monarchies of the region as soon as oil wealth is no longer able to buy off discontent.

Already beyond the power of established Islam and the non-Islamic world, there is meanwhile another force not merely threatening but inflicting chaos through powerful rogue terrorist groups in a widening sphere of different territories. There is no knowing where tomorrow's bombs will be detonated in destroying the peaceful and innocent. The threat of fundamentalism to world civilisation would be met by the emergence of a new intolerance from all quarters in meeting these assaults, and the consequent loss of freedom, followed by an intellectual paralysis, and the general curtailment of material and moral progress in all societies.

In view of the dangers cited above, it must be a first priority to divert our politicians in their exasperation from tending towards the plea, like Cato the Censor, at the end of every speech in the Senate, irrespective of the subject under debate, *"Ceterum censeo Carthaginem esse delendam,"*[18] the awful reality of which occurred just three years after his death. That would be the worst of all possibilities but in an unpredictable world, as we find today, it would not remain entirely inconceivable.

The irony is that all this mischief stems from the accidental overflowing of malignant Wahabism from the Saudi state, and the latter is unable to stem the tide whilst also confronting the quite separate issue of the Shia threat on its various frontiers. The tragedy is that if the Saudi and other Gulf states collapse in anarchy they are unlikely to receive much sympathy from the non-Islamic world due to malign forces originally traceable to their own responsibility but now clearly out of their control.

---

[18] "Moreover, I advise that Carthage must be destroyed."

Select Bibliography

Binder, Leonard, *Islamic Liberalism: A critique of Development Ideologies*, Chicago Univ. Press, 1988.

Bowen, John, *A New Anthropology of Islam*, CUP, 2012

Burgat, François, *Face to Face with Political Islam*, I.B. Taurus, 2005.

Carter, Geoff, *Death in Riyadh: dark secrets in hidden Arabia*, Arena Books, 2000.

Corfe, Robert, *Deism & Social Ethics: the role of religion in the third millennium*, Arena Books, 2007.

Corfe, Robert, *The Democratic Imperative: the reality of power relationships in the Nation State*, Arena Books, 2013.

Dawson, Christopher, *Progress & Religion: an historical enquiry*, Sheed & Ward, 1929.

Fandy, Mamoun, *Saudi Arabia & the Politics of Dissent*, St. Martin's Press, NY, 1999.

Gerges, Fawaz, *America & Political Islam: Clash of Cultures or Clash of Interests*, CUP, 1999.

Gray, John, *Black Mass: Apolcalyptic Religion & the Death of Utopia*, Penguin, 2007.

Haykel, Bernard, et al (eds.), *Saudi Arabia in Transiation: Insights on Social, Political, Economic & Religious change*, CUP, 2015.

Heffelfinger, Chris, *Radical Islam in America: Salafism's Journey from Arabia to the West*, Potomac Books, Washington DC, 2011.

Hegghammer, Thomas, *Jihad in Saudi Arabia: Violence & Pan-Islamism since 1979*, CUP, 2010.

Hobhouse, L.T., *Morals in Evolution, A study in Comparative Ethics*, Henry Holt, NY, 3rd ed., 1915.

Huxley, Julian, *Religion Without Revelation*, Max Parrish, 1957.

Ismail, Salwa, *Political Life in Cairo's New Quarters: Encountering the Everyday State*, Minnesota Univ. Press, 2006.

Kechichian, Joseph, *Legal & Political Reforms in Saudi Arabia,*
    Routledge, 2013.
Kepel, Gilles, *Jihad: The Trial of Political Islam*, I.B, Taurus,
    2003.
Kurtman, Charles (ed.), *Modernist Islam: a source book*, OUP,
    2002.
Lacroix, Stephanie, *Awakening Islam: Religious Dissent in
    Contemporary Saudi Arabia*, Harvard UP, 2011.
Laurence, Bruce, *Defenders of God: The Fundamentalist Revolt
    Against the Modern Age*, S. Carolina UP, 2006.
Martin, Richard & Barzegar, Abbas (eds.), *Islamism: Contested
    Perpsectives on Politcal Islam*, Stanford UP, 2010.
Marthiesen, Toby, *The Other Saudis: Shiism, Dissent &
    Sectarianism*, CUP, 2015.
Massad, Joseph, *Islam in Liberalism*, Univ. of Chicago Press,
    2015.
Meijer, Roel (ed.), *Global Salafism, Islam's New Religious
    Movement*, Hurst & Co., 2009.
Morozov, Eugeny, *The Net Delusion: How not to Liberate the
    World*, Allen Lane, 2011.
Pankhurst, Reza, *The Inevitable Caliphate? A history of the
    Struggle for Global Islamic Union, 1924 to the Present*,
    Hurst & Co., 2013.
Rasheed, Al-, Madawi, *Muted Modernists: The Struggle over
    Divine Politics in Saudi Arabia*, Hurdst & Co., 2015.
Rasheed, Al-, Madawi, *Contesting the Saudi State: Islamic
    Voices from a New Generaton*, CUP, 2007.
Rasheed, Al-, Madawi, *A History of Saudi Arabia*, 2nd ed.,
    CUP, 2010.
Rasheed, Al-, Madawi, *A most Masculine State: Gender,
    Religion & Politics in Saudi Arabia,* CUP, 2013.
Rasheed, Al-, Madawi, et al (eds.), *Demystifying the Caliphate:
    Historical memory & contemporary contexts,* Hurst &
    Co., 2012.
Roy, Olivier, *Holy Ignorance: When Religion & Culture Part
    Ways*, Hurst & Co., 2010.

Thompson, Mark, *Saudi Arabia & the Path to Political Change: National Dialogue & Civil Society*, I.B. Taurus, 2014.
Toynbee, Arnold, *A Study of History*, OUP, 1955/1960 eds., 12 vols.
Tukor, M.A.R., *Past & Future of Ethics*, OUP, 1938.

INDEX

Lightning Source UK Ltd.
Milton Keynes UK
UKOW03f1525180416

272459UK00002B/238/P